Regarding Agnes

CATHY FRENCH

CALLING BIRD BOOKS

Calling Bird Books

First published in Great Britain by Calling Bird Books, 2025

Copyright © 2025 Cathy French

ISBN: 978-1-0683477-0-2

To Tina, Ron and (most of all) Dad

The little boy lost in the lonely fen,
Led by the wandering light,
Began to cry, but God, ever nigh,
Appeared like a father in white.

He kissed the child, and by the hand led,
And to his mother brought,
Who in sorrow pale, through the lonely dale,
Her little boy weeping sought.

'The Little Boy Found' from W. Blake's *Songs of Innocence*

FAMILY TREES

The Smiths and The Gortons

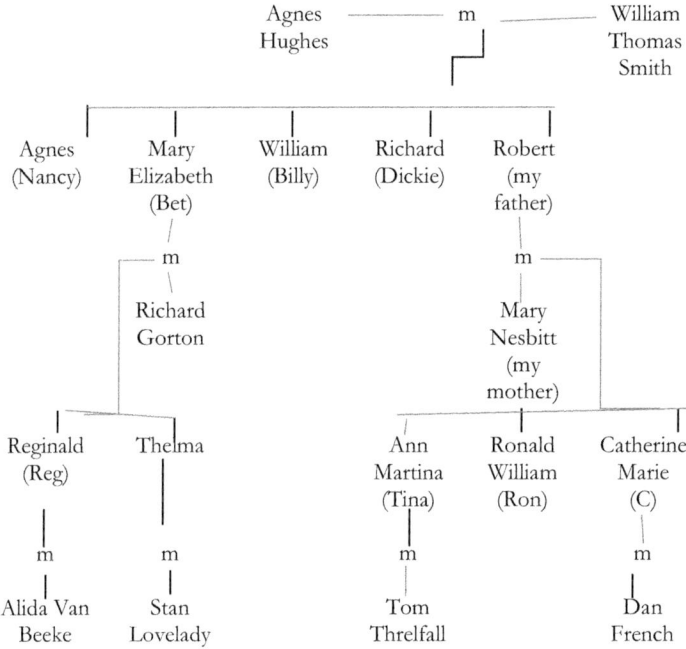

The Nesbitts

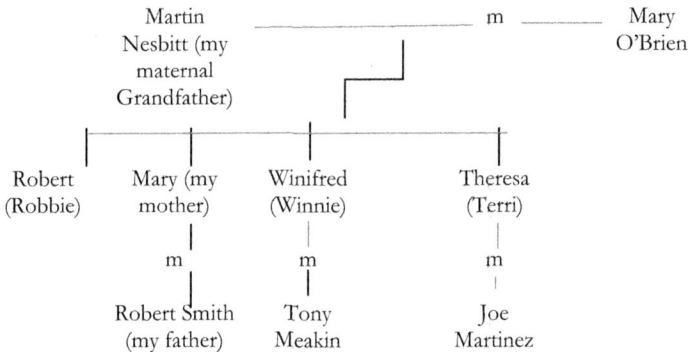

Martin Nesbitt (my maternal Grandfather) ——————— m ——————— Mary O'Brien

Robert (Robbie)

Mary (my mother)
m
Robert Smith (my father)

Winifred (Winnie)
m
Tony Meakin

Theresa (Terri)
m
Joe Martinez

CONTENTS

The Envelope

Dear Dad,

I found an envelope last night. It was brown and age-battered, and on the front where the address should go you'd written in block capitals MARRIAGE CERTS, SERVICE DISCHARGE BOOK, BIRTH CERTIFICATES, MY MUMS MAIDEN NAME. I don't recall seeing it before, although I must have been given it when we were clearing out your flat. And inside (as stated) was your birth certificate, Mum's birth certificate, your wedding certificate, your army service book, and a scrap of lined paper torn from a jotter bearing a single, half-forgotten name: Agnes Hughes.

C

16

Dear Dad,

You spoke sparingly about your childhood. The bits and pieces I collected can be rendered within a few sentences. Your father, William Smith, was killed in action in World War One – you never knew him. Your mother, Agnes, died of a broken heart, you were told. Your childhood was mostly spent in Dr Barnardo's orphanages separated from your four older siblings, Nancy, Bet, Billy, and Dickie.

You never spoke to me about William, yet my dead grandfather held a special place in my heart. From the moment Mum showed me his name in the Roll of Honour at Liverpool Town Hall, I was captivated by the idea of him. He was a war hero, as I saw it, part of that beautiful, lost generation of men who didn't return from the carnage wrought between 1914 and 1918. He looked out at me from the sepia images in school textbooks. He spoke to me through the poetry of Rupert Brooke and Wilfred Owen. His name lived on through my brother, Ronald William.

In contrast to William, Agnes Smith, your mother, was as insubstantial as air. She was not my grandmother in the way William was my grandfather. There was nothing about her to grasp hold of; each time I tried she slipped through my fingers. Her name wasn't on public display and nor was it passed down to Tina or to me; no one had written a poem about her; no one had published her photograph in a book. If I thought of her at all it was as a rather pathetic figure, pining and fading for her doomed husband, like a minor character in a minor Victorian novel, although I didn't honestly believe a woman could die of a broken heart. Perhaps neither did you but it was all you had to offer.

Now, holding the scrap of paper between my finger and thumb, time slips. I'm nine years old, ten maybe, interviewing you for a school project. You tell me that the day your mother died was one of the saddest in your life. Remembering that and seeing her name in black and white, Agnes begins to coalesce. She takes on a shape, a form, a reality: she is a mother bringing up children alone in a time of war, a wife not knowing if she will ever see her husband again, and still further back, before she was wife and mother, she is a young girl called Agnes Hughes.

Why did you write down her name and file it with your documents? It might not have been your intention but you've sparked my curiosity. I've decided to do some digging. I'm going to find out what became of Agnes Hughes.

C

Back to the Beginning (1905 to 1926)

Dear Dad,
Before Lord Kitchener sent William Smith to war, Agnes's life was unremarkable.

Agnes Hughes was born in 1879, the middle child of Robert and Mary-Jane Hughes. Until she married she lived at 82 Smeaton Street, Kirkdale, Liverpool, with her widowed mother, siblings Eliza Ann and Charles, and half-brothers William and Robert Beattie from Mary-Jane's earlier marriage. She was working as a domestic servant, the most common female occupation at that time.

She married aged twenty-four – the average age for women then. The groom, William Thomas Smith, a general labourer, was twenty-eight. They were wed on 16 April 1905 at St Mary's Church, Kirkdale. Eliza Ann and William Beattie acted as witnesses.

Agnes begins life as Mrs William Thomas Smith at 41 Smeaton Street, close to her family home. The couple didn't have to wait long for their first child. Nancy is born on 2 April 1906, less than a year after the wedding. By then the young family have moved to 20 Hibbert Street.

Three years later, Agnes and William have another girl. Bet arrives on 1 May 1909. They are now living at 52 Bismarck Street. Somewhere along the way they had a child who did not survive: the 1911 census indicates three children, two living and one dead.

Their first son, Billy, is born on 7 November 1911. They have moved yet again, to 24 Spurgeon Street. This is where they will finally settle, the house you called home.

It's another five years before Dickie appears on 24 June 1916. By then Gavilo Princep had fired his gun and changed the world. Dickie's birth certificate gives William's occupation as Private (2615) South Lancs (General Labourer). This is where normal life begins to unravel.

Two years later Agnes gives birth to her fifth and final child, Robert, on 10 October 1918. You were a war baby, Dad. I'd never considered it before now.

C

Dear Dad,
I've retraced Agnes and William's footsteps as far as possible to try to put flesh on the dry bones of old dates.

St Mary's Church, where Agnes and William were married, stood on Walton Road. Unfortunately it closed in 1973 and was demolished in 1979, less than 150 years after it was built. Where it once stood is an ugly, squat, square building housing a Citizen's Advice Bureau next to a strip of tarmac acting as the CAB car park. I visited on a Sunday when I knew the CAB would be closed and sat in my car, trying to blot out the current structure and resurrect the handsome, red-brick Victorian church I'd seen in photographs online. Next to the car park, set back from the road, there's a small park, which might once have been the graveyard to the church. Nowadays it's a hangout for the local youths, judging by the empty Kronenburg cans discarded in the grass near the railings.

Smeaton Street, where Agnes lived with her birth-family and began married life with William, is now mostly made up of new-build bungalows, but Agnes's mother's home, number 82, is unmistakeably Victorian so it must be the actual building where she once lived. Number 41, her first marital home, is still standing too. The street is shaped like a shepherd's crook and though the numbers would seem to suggest otherwise number 41 is directly opposite number 82 – so Agnes began her married life right across the road from her old family home. I picture her waving to her mother, Mary-Jane, from the front room.

I eventually managed to find Hibbert Street, Bismarck Street and Spurgeon Street on an OS street map from 1960. The streets themselves no longer exist, demolished around 1969 with the surrounding roads. A tiny part of Spurgeon Street, where Agnes and William finally settled, the place you called home, lives on as Spurgeon Close, a neat cul-de-sac of new build houses and bungalows, very different from the two-up-two-down terrace you described.

Comparing the 1960 map with the modern version it's striking just how few roads remain. Immediately surrounding Spurgeon Street, an area of less than one mile, there once stood:

Danby Street
Elmore Street
Lance Street
Eastlake Street
Jasmine Street
Desmond Street
Moreland Street
Creswick Street
Copley Street
Poplar Street

– all gone.

A small hop across Hamilton Road, where Bismarck Street used to stand, is now the site of Breckfield Community Comprehensive. The same site also housed:

Friar Street
Abbot Street
Priory Street
Orient Street
Priory Grove
Clarence Grove
Church Place
Monk Street
Eyes Street
Cowl Street.

A short stroll to the end of Hamilton Road would once have brought you within quarter of a mile of Hibbert Street and also:

Kepler Street
Sampson Street
Jefferson Street
Waterhouse Street
Abbey Street
Stonewall Street
Copeland Street
St Georges Hill
Amos Street
Minerva Street
Samuel Street
Priory Road
Fairy Street
Mount Joy Street
Magnum Street
Mitford Street
Mitford Walk
Mitford Close

Priory Mount
Priory Hill
Seville Street
Patmos Street
Cicero Terrace
Daniel Street
Joshua Street
Ewbank Street
Pyramid Street
Caros Street.

There was a cinema, and John Bagot Hospital. It's the same story on the next block,
and the next,
and the next.

No wonder you never wanted to go back. You wouldn't have recognised the place.

I wanted to see what the old area looked like and managed to find a searchable photographic archive of lost Everton streets on the internet. I was expecting to see rows of tenements, little more than slums, but street name after street name brought up photographs of solid, Victorian terraces, the kind still popular today. The biggest revelation, though, was the community. There are photographs of neighbours chatting on the threshold of their homes, street parties, a May Day parade, corner shops, a thriving high-street. It seemed so full of life and love.

I tried to see Agnes in the women scrubbing their doorsteps and William in the men in flat caps. But whatever clues I'm looking for won't be found in maps of long-lost streets and photographs of places that no longer exist. It's like trying to chase an echo or catch a shadow.

That was probably another reason you never went back to the area. There was little point; the answer to what happened to Agnes is not there.
C

Dear Dad,
The turning point in Agnes's story was World War One.

It is 28 June 1914. At this point Agnes and William Smith have three children: Nancy (eight), Bet (six) and Billy (two). You are in the future; so is Dickie. It will be another fifty years before Liverpool Council take a wrecking ball to Spurgeon Street. On the face of it the Smiths at number 24 have a perfectly ordinary marriage and are thriving.

****

One thousand five hundred miles away from Liverpool, the citizens of Sarajevo are welcoming Archduke Franz Ferdinand, the heir to the Austrian-Hungarian throne, for an official visit to the city – though not everyone on the streets watching the Duke's motorcade is a fan.

Gavrilo Princep, a nineteen year old Bosnian Serb, takes a gun from his coat and shoots at the Archduke's car, killing him and his wife. Princep must have realised there was no coming back from this: he must have known he would be caught, convicted, and die in gaol. What Princep could not have foreseen was the chain of events he set in motion; how his bullets would ricochet around the world, acting as wrecking balls to the lives of innocent people thousands of miles away in places he'd never been and barely dreamed of. Around forty million people worldwide would not come back from this.

A month after the assassination, on 4 August 1914, Britain declares war on Germany. Our professional army is too small to take on the mighty German forces, so Lord Kitchener, the newly made Secretary of State for War, is suddenly everywhere, his face glaring accusingly from posters proclaiming YOUR COUNTRY NEEDS YOU! It's an appeal to manly patriotism, a call to join a new citizens' army.

William finds he has no beef with the Kaiser any more than he does with the King and in any case, he is thirty-eight and fighting is a game for younger men. His conscience is clear: his country might need him but so do his wife and kids. His country will have to make do without him.

It takes a little under two years for the decision to be taken out of his hands. With casualties mounting and volunteers drying up there is talk of enforced conscription. People are sceptical – it had never been done before and wouldn't wash now – but in January 1916 the Military Services Act is passed, introducing conscription for single men aged eighteen to forty-one.

As a married man William is not caught in the net – or not at first. In May 1916 a second Military Services Act is passed, applying to all men aged eighteen to forty-one regardless of marital status. War has finally caught up with William. Agnes is distraught: she is eight months pregnant with their fourth child.

William was forty when he was conscripted. I'd like to think he got to hold his new-born son, Dickie, born on 24 June 1916, before he was shipped off to God knows where. Dickie wouldn't miss him; Nancy (ten), Bet (seven), and Billy (four) would. Agnes would have to deal with the fallout.

C

Dear Dad,

How Agnes survived the war is a matter of supposition. When William was conscripted the family lost its only breadwinner. Agnes almost certainly wouldn't have been employed: in 1916 it was frowned upon for married women to work and for Agnes, a mother, it would be doubly unacceptable because she would be seen as neglecting her children.

From the time William was conscripted the family would have lived on a separation allowance from the War Office. Allowances were generally eleven shillings per week for the wife and one shilling per child, meaning Agnes would receive a total of fifteen shillings, say. To put this in context, a report into wages by the War Emergency Workers' National Committee found that unskilled general labourers were earning an absolute minimum of eighteen shillings a week and some working class men were earning as much as sixty shillings a week. With William away there would be some, small savings, the weekly food bill would reduce a little, but most large outgoings – rent, coal, shoes for the children – would be unaffected. Even assuming William's pay was at the lower end of the scale, Agnes was faced with a seventeen per cent reduction in the family's income at best; at worst the drop would be much greater.

If Agnes found it tough to balance the reduced family budget, she'd soon have a more pressing concern: finding anything to eat. By 1917 the country was running out of food. The weather conspired with the war and turned a bad situation worse. It rained, and rained, and rained, and rained again. Heaven was weeping for the world. Bad weather plus lack of men equalled a difficult harvest. Fields were transformed into marshland; crops rotted in the sodden ground. Basic foodstuffs like potatoes and bread, which poorer households like Agnes's would rely on, became increasingly scarce.

In February 1917, Liverpool Market reported a ninety per cent drop in potato stocks (twenty tons compared to their usual two hundred tons). By July 1917 Liverpool Council had opened two food kitchens. I picture Agnes leaving the house in Spurgeon Street, walking down Hamilton Road towards Heyworth Street, and then from street to street for a mile or so before reaching the nearest kitchen at Day Industrial School in Addison Street. Given the weather that year, the walking would have been wet. Rainwater would seep through any holes in the soles of her shoes, soaking her feet. I see the children at home, Nancy rocking baby Dickie, Bet playing with toddler Billy, waiting for Agnes to return with a family meal of potatoes and gravy (cost: sixpence). When Agnes could afford a few pence more there might even be meat.

By 1918 the food situation was dire. The mortality rate for poor children was one in four. Agnes beat the odds, though; she kept herself and her brood alive.

It's what happened after the War that I need to unscramble.

C

Dear Dad,

I recently went back to take another look at the Roll of Honour in Liverpool Town Hall. It must be nearly fifty years since I last saw it, when Mum took me there as a little girl. I remember it took a long time to find William's name, and now I understand why. The Roll is not in simple alphabetical order and there are a lot of names to read – more than thirteen thousand men from Liverpool and the surrounding districts lost their lives in World War One. These days there is an online search tool so I already knew to head for Panel 41, Right, and there he was: PTE. W.T. SMITH, SOUTH LANCASHIRE REGT.

No one seems to know when or how William died, exactly. All we know for sure is that he died in active service. The fact you were born in October 1918 means William must have survived until January 1918, nine months before. Soldiers were given leave every eighteen months or so, and if William was shipped out the month after Dickie was born, in July 1916 say, he'd be due leave in January 1918. The dates seem to fit. That would place William's death sometime between January 1918 and Armistice on 30 November 1918.

If I'm struggling to pinpoint the 'when' of William's death, the 'where' and 'how' are proving equally elusive. Tina remembers being told he was lost at sea, Ron thinks he died during the 1918 Spanish flu epidemic. They could both be right. The first wave of Spanish flu peaked in spring 1918, followed by a second, deadlier wave in the summer. Troopships were perfect breeding grounds for the virus with men crammed together in close quarters and quarantine not strictly enforced. There are stories of apparently healthy soldiers boarding ships, only to fall sick and die within a day or two: a short illness but long enough to pass on the virus to their shipmates. It is possible William succumbed to flu when he was being transported to a new combat zone or being transported home.

Autumn 1918 must have been an especially fraught time for Agnes: five children, including a new-born baby, her husband dead and a deadly virus on the doorstep. You might not realise it, Dad, but you were lucky to survive through to infancy. You were pushed into the world when Spanish flu was sweeping the country. Only a few weeks after you were born on 10 October 1918, Liverpool recorded its first case. Barely a week later there were over two hundred confirmed deaths in the city. When news of Armistice broke ecstatic people filled the streets regardless of Government advice to avoid crowds. The advice was probably useless anyway. Troops were being sent home, spreading the virus as they went. By the time you celebrated your second birthday Spanish flu had killed fifty million people worldwide, about ten per cent of the population at the time, twenty-five per cent more than were killed in the entirety of World War One.

Can you remember the fear it engendered? Four years of war and food shortages and now this...plague. It must have seemed as if death and destruction would continue forever. C

Dear Dad,

By November 1918 Agnes would have received a letter from the War Office. She wouldn't need to read it: the tell-tale black-edged envelope would be enough. Other women in the neighbourhood would have received the same.

When the letter arrived Agnes would have felt...what? Grief-stricken? Numb? She was probably numb anyway from just trying to survive, and without a body, a coffin, a funeral, news of William's death might have seemed like another unreal element of the unreal situation she was forced to navigate. In any case Agnes could not have afforded to lose herself in grief; the practical matter of money once more required her attention.

She would continue to receive the separation allowance for a year after William's death at which point it would stop and be replaced by a war widow's pension...in theory. In practice the transition from allowance to pension was subject to a tortuous application process.

Pension application forms would have been attached to the letter informing Agnes of William's death. As well as completing the forms, Agnes would have to send copies of her marriage certificate and her children's birth certificates. As a minimum (assuming you weren't yet born) that would be five certificates at three shillings per copy, a total of fifteen shillings. The paperwork alone would cost her a whole week's income. It wasn't something that could be done quickly; she would need to budget and plan to set money aside. (How will she feed the children, how will she pay the rent?)

On top of finding the money to apply, Agnes would need a police officer or a Justice of the Peace to complete a declaration vouching for the accuracy of the information and for her character as being in every respect deserving of the grant of a pension. If a document is missing the application will be delayed or rejected; if she makes a mistake filling in the form, the application will be delayed or rejected.

Even after jumping through all those hoops, Agnes was not guaranteed any money. The War Office viewed the widow's pension as reward for a husband's service, not as a widow's right. If William was judged to have died due to his own negligence or misconduct, Agnes would receive nothing.

Given the long-winded, hit-and-miss system for obtaining a war widow's pension, Agnes would need a back-up plan to prevent the family starving when the separation allowance ceased. In 1918 the welfare state was in its infancy. There was no child benefit or universal credit for Agnes to fall back on. Eminent politicians (including Liverpool-born William Rathbone) opposed the poor having an absolute right to relief, arguing it encouraged passivity and dependency.

Agnes's only option would be to appeal for charitable relief from parish funds. Going 'on the parish' was considered shameful. Bodies in charge of administering the funds, the Charity Organisation Society and the local Boards of Guardians, were extremely judgemental, enforcing strict ideas about self-help and making distinctions between the deserving poor and the undeserving poor. Applicants were as likely to be offered a closed fist as an open hand.

If a claimant was regarded as deserving, an inspector would visit them every week to check on their sobriety, good conduct and cleanliness, which added to the stigma. The parish system was better than its precursor, the workhouse system – but not by much.

I imagine Agnes resented the weekly visits but submitted, subsuming whatever pride remained to the more pressing need of putting food on the table.

What I'm yet to discover is how long the hand-to-mouth existence of living 'on the parish' continued and how or when Agnes died.

C

Dear Dad,

I found a clue to when Agnes died in an old scrapbook.

You might not remember much about that school project I worked on when I was nine or ten. The concept was simple: ask family members fifteen questions about themselves. I took the interviews very seriously, making rough notes in a jotter then writing up the responses in my best handwriting. I pasted the finished transcripts into a large, white scrapbook purchased specially for the project. Forty-five years and ten house moves later, I still have that scrapbook.

The questions are a mixture of factual (when were you born; where did you live) and reminiscence (what was school like; what do you remember as the saddest time of your life). You answered question five 'What did you do as a child?' with: 'Spent most of childhood in Dr Barnardo's Orphanage (aged six to thirteen)'.

If you were six when you went into the orphanage it would put Agnes's year of death as 1924 or 1925. Her marriage certificate from April 1905 gives her age as twenty-four, which makes her birth-year 1880 or 1881.

And so I spent an evening with a bottle of wine and an ancestry website, searching online records. There was an Agnes Smith from Lancashire whose dates matched – born 1881, died 1924 – but she was from Bolton, not Liverpool, so she can't be your mother.

Then I spotted some confusion or contradiction around the year Agnes was born. The 1911 census, taken in April that year, shows Agnes as aged thirty, which is consistent with her being born in 1880 or 1881, whereas the 1901 census taken in March 1901 states her age as twenty-two, which would make her birth year a couple of years' earlier, 1878 or 1879. The 1901 census predates her marriage to William. Could Agnes have knocked two years off her age when she met him? Would that even be possible?

I widened the search criteria. It yielded another two Agnes Smiths, both from the right registration area, West Derby. One is clearly not a match (born 1877, died 1928); the other is a match for the birth year (born 1880) but died in 1929, which would make you ten or eleven when she died, so she can't be your mother either.

Nothing seems to fit, Dad, but I won't give up. People don't simply disappear. Agnes must be somewhere in the records. I'll find her.

If she's looking down on me from somewhere perhaps she can point the way. Agnes, give me a sign, a clue; show yourself. What happened to you?

C

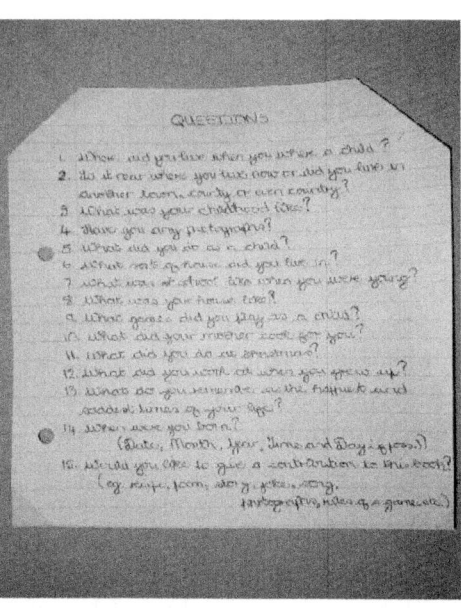

QUESTIONS

1. Where did you live when you were a child?
2. Is it near where you live now or did you live in another town, county or even country?
3. What was your childhood like?
4. Have you any photographs?
5. What did you do as a child?
6. What sort of house did you live in?
7. What was it about life when you were young?
8. What was your home like?
9. What games did you play as a child?
10. What did your mother cook for you?
11. What did you do at Christmas?
12. What did you want to be when you grew up?
13. What do you remember as the happiest and saddest times of your life?
14. When were you born?
    (Date, Month, Year, Time and Day if poss.)
15. Would you like to give a contribution to this book?
    (eg. recipe, poem, story, joke, song.
        photographs, rules of a game etc.)

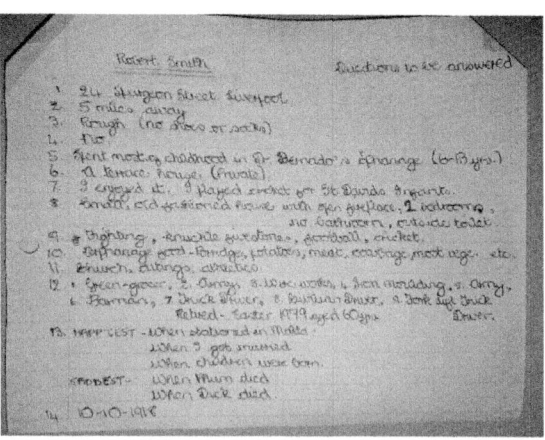

Robert Smith   Questions to be answered

1. 24 Sturgeon Street, Liverpool.
2. 5 miles away
3. Rough (no shoes or socks)
4. No
5. Spent most of childhood in Dr Barndo's Exchange (6-15yrs.)
6. A terrace house (private)
7. I enjoyed it. I played cricket for St Bando's Infants.
8. Small, old fashioned house with open fireplace, 2 bedrooms, no bathroom, outside toilet
9. Fighting, knuckle questions, football, cricket.
10. Exchange food - porridge, potatoes, meat, cabbage, root veg. etc.
11. church, outings, athletics
12. 1. Green-grocer, 2. Army, 3.Window washer, 4. Farm labouring, 5. Army, 6. Barman, 7.Truck driver, 8. Builder's labour, 9. Fork lift truck
    Retired - Easter 1979 aged 60yrs.   Driver.
13. HAPPIEST - When stationed in Malta
               When I got married
               When children were born.
    SADDEST - When Mum died
              When Dick died
14. 10-10-1918

Barnardo's, Liverpool (1926 to 1928)

Dear Dad,

I applied to Barnardo's for your records. I thought they might shed some light on what became of Agnes.

As far as I can recall you never told me where the Liverpool orphanage was sited. Perhaps you never knew the exact location; after all you were only a child when they took you in. It was on the corner of Myrtle Street and Sugnall Street.

You barely went into the city centre that I can remember so you might not know where that is. From the Pier Head, with your back towards the Liver Building, head towards the main shopping area. Walk up Church Street, past the entrance to Liverpool One, and keep walking, past the bombed out shell of St Luke's church until you reach the Philharmonic pub. Diagonally opposite you'll see the Art Deco facade of the Philharmonic Hall – you might remember coming here for my graduation ceremony. The obvious way from here is to turn onto Hope Street, left towards the crown-shaped Metropolitan Cathedral (Paddy's Wigwam) or right towards the Anglican Cathedral. Instead, cross over the junction and carry on down Myrtle Street.

You're looking for number 2A, a large red-brick building on the right hand side of Myrtle Street, just after Sugnall Street. It's a Victorian building, reassuringly solid but with no obvious architectural merit compared to other buildings in the city. It doesn't particularly stand out in this area or in this street even, despite being Grade II listed.

For a better view cross Myrtle Street and stand at the bus stop on the opposite side. From here you'll be able to take in the ornate, gilt lettering on the facade between the ground level and first floor windows. The gold colour stands out beautifully against the red-brick and the words are easily legible. You might remember. It reads:

The SHELTERING HOME for DESTITUTE CHILDREN

You said you were taken into care at the age of six but Barnardo's records show you were admitted in May 1926, so you were actually slightly older, seven. The Liverpool Sheltering Home was the first of four Dr Barnardo's homes you were sent to. You lived here almost two years.

Standing at the bus stop looking at the gilt lettering, for the first time I began to wonder how it felt as a small boy, aged seven, separated from everything and everyone you know, coming face to face with this lofty facade. Myrtle Street lies only two miles from where your home in Spurgeon Street once stood but that small terrace house must have seemed a million miles away.

Your siblings, too, were gone. By May 1926 your two sisters, Nancy and Bet, now aged twenty and seventeen, were working as live-in domestic servants, Nancy in Oxford Street and Bet in Elizabeth Street. Your eldest brother, Billy, fourteen, school leaving age at the time, was at Holy Trinity Industrial School, a kind of boarding school for paupers, being prepared for future employment. Dickie, aged nine, was sent to live in Wales.

That always struck me as the cruelest thing of all, that you were separated from your brothers.

You came here alone.

It's probably as well you didn't know it would be over forty years before you and Dickie met once more, or that you'd never see Nancy or Billy ever again. It would have been bleak enough already, being led up the small flight of steps and into that austere, red-brick building, without that knowledge weighing you down even further. I imagine you would have felt sad, lonely, bewildered, and perhaps a little scared; trying to work out what you'd done wrong, for what unspecified transgression you were being punished.

I would have liked to have looked inside but there is no public access. The bulk of the building is now given over to student accommodation – on the day of my visit the railings were draped with a large banner publicising rooms – although there's a fine dining restaurant in the basement with a separate entrance on Sugnall Street, called The Art School Restaurant, a nod to Liverpool Art School, which occupied the building later; better for business than The Sheltering Home Restaurant, I expect. To the rear of the building is a small concrete courtyard, which might have been your playground, now mostly taken up by a new Orangery-type extension to the restaurant.

Back home again, I found some information about the inside of building on the Historic England website. Despite some internal alteration it seems it is still possible to read the original interior. There were large open-plan dormitories; classrooms and dining hall to the rear; smaller classrooms, offices and officers' quarters to the front. But I don't need to tell you – you lived there. You might be glad (or not) to learn that decorative tiling depicting English Kings and Queens still survives.

C

Dear Dad,

I always found it strange that you nursed a hatred of Dr Barnardo's; refused to countenance anyone in the family donating money to the charity, even seven decades after you left. Reading recollections of people who grew up in the homes, I'm beginning to understand why.

Life was governed by a strict timetable. If Liverpool Sheltering Home was typical, you would have slept in a dormitory and been woken by a bell at 6.30am or 7.00am. You would make your bed, say prayers, wash in cold water, get dressed, and be inspected before being allowed breakfast. After breakfast, it was time for the toilet (bowel movement expected or syrup of figs from matron) and then lessons. There was playtime (outside, whatever the weather). There was dinner, tea, and bed. There was church on Sundays. It was routine, not necessarily a bad thing in itself, but it wasn't normal family life. Visits from family were generally discouraged, although some homes allowed an hour-long visit once a month. Did Liverpool Sheltering Home allow visits? You never mentioned anyone visiting you – but then, you said very little about life in the orphanage.

The more I think about it, the more I realise the irony of having a fine dining restaurant in a former orphanage, not least because mealtimes feature a lot in the recollections.

The food itself wasn't a problem. It wasn't *Oliver Twist*; you weren't starved. The things you remembered eating – porridge for breakfast, meat and vegetables for dinner followed by rice pudding, bread and jam and cocoa for tea – seem child-friendly and wholesome; similar to the food I was given to eat at that age. You probably ate more, and better, in Dr Barnardo's than you ever did at home in Spurgeon Street.

The issue was more with the regime around mealtimes. I have a grainy black and white photograph titled 'Ready for a Meal: A View of the Dining Hall' from a copy of the Liverpool Sheltering Home's newsletter *Night and Day*. It shows children seated on benches, six to a table. At the head of each table is a school master, wearing a suit and tie. The children are all in uniform, boys in suits, girls in dresses and pinafores. Boys and girls are on separate tables. It looks very stiff and formal.

You remembered having to eat all the food on your plate or you'd be force-fed at the table. Talking wasn't allowed. Mealtimes weren't a time for cementing friendships and learning social skills, they were a functional exercise in refuelling, at best; at worst an endurance test.

Silence extended beyond mealtimes. There was no talking in the corridors; you would have been marched silently in crocodiles between rooms.

The thread connecting every story, the unspoken subtext, is not living conditions, or routine, or food: it's the absence of love.

You remembered having soap put in your mouth for speaking out of turn; getting a belt across the bare bottom for being naughty. Some alumni of the homes recall these and other, harsher punishments: a hairbrush on the back of the hand; being stood on top of a fragile-looking glass cover over a high stairwell. There are accounts of lumps and welts that lasted a month.

I was hit – by you, by Mum – supposedly to instil the difference between right and wrong (could you have done that without hitting?) but I was also kissed, hugged and cuddled. There are no stories of cuddles, or hugs, or kind words in the alumni accounts. The aim of residential childcare in the 1920s was to instil moral fibre and prepare for employment, not provide happy memories. Discipline, education, and religious instruction were the key, in accordance with Victorian principles of 'spare the rod and spoil the child' and 'children should be seen, not heard'. It was less about caring for children than about training them as future citizens; emotions didn't enter the equation.

To be fair, to the same attitude prevailed in public schools. It was cold and loveless. No wonder you tried to run away.

They caught you and brought you back. You didn't tell me the consequences.

C

Dear Dad,

I've noticed the admission history describes you as a 'bright boy, but delicate'. Your record book shows you were admitted to hospital with chicken pox six months after moving into the home and back in hospital again less than a year later.

The hospital they sent you to would have been the Children's Infirmary, which was also in Myrtle Street. The main Infirmary was on Myrtle Street, too, as well as a Cancer Hospital, a Lying-In Hospital, and an Eye and Ear Infirmary. Perhaps the Liverpool Sheltering Home building doesn't stand out from the rest of the buildings in the street because so many of them were built for similar purposes. It might also explain why so many buildings in that part of the city are now being used by universities and colleges: institution is baked into their bricks.

Your sickliness could well have been a blessing in disguise. It turns out Liverpool Sheltering Home was at the centre of a radical scheme to send destitute children to Canada.

The instigator behind the scheme was not Dr Barnardo but a woman called Louisa Birt. For Louisa (and other like-minded people) the scheme was simple, yet brilliant. England had surplus children, street kids with no shoes or socks; Canada hadn't enough hands to work the land. It was a match made in heaven.

Louisa had started the resettlement scheme in London in the 1870s with her sister Annie McPherson. They didn't restrict themselves to children who were genuinely orphaned. Children of widows who were unable to support them, or of drunken or violent fathers, were also considered as legitimate candidates for Canada. When Louisa was passing through Liverpool with a batch of Canadian-bound London children – Liverpool was Britain's principal port of embarkation for emigrants to the New World at the time – she was persuaded that the same kind of project could be beneficial in Liverpool, too.

It was Louisa who established Liverpool Sheltering Home in 1873, originally in a different building on Myrtle Street, before moving in 1889 into the newer, larger premises at number 2A. Annie had established a Distributing House in Ontario. In a typical year around two hundred children would be shipped from Myrtle Street to the distribution agent in Canada.

Louisa remained as superintendent of Liverpool Sheltering Home until her death in 1915, when her daughter, Lillian, took over. In 1925, the year before you were admitted, Liverpool Sheltering Home amalgamated with Dr Barnardo's.

Dr Barnardo's at the time was already well-acquainted with emigration schemes. In the 1870s Dr Thomas Barnardo used the services of Annie and Louisa to organise the migration of children from his homes before starting up his own emigration scheme in 1882. By 1925 the Barnardo's schemes were extensive. Dr B's pledge never to turn away a destitute child – the famous ever open door policy – required an ever open exit door too.

It was precisely the extent of the Barnardo's schemes that made it so attractive to Liverpool Sheltering Home. The April 1925 copy of *Night and Day* makes it clear that Liverpool Sheltering Home approached the Council of Dr. Barnardo's because the aims and principles of the two organisations were identical. The home saw it as a way to continue and expand their emigration work. Little surprise, then, that after amalgamation Liverpool Sheltering Home continued operating as a migration and training centre, although due to changes in Canadian law only boys over fourteen could now be 'distributed'.

Despite periodic concerns about the welfare, treatment, and monitoring of migrated children, by the time it closed in 1935 Liverpool Sheltering Home had shipped almost eight thousand children aged from two to seventeen years old to be resettled with families in Canada.

You didn't mention the migrations at all. It's likely you knew nothing of them. On 24 April 1928, less than two years after your admission into Liverpool Sheltering Home, you were on the move again. You were on your way to Clapham.

C

Clapham and Hove (1928 to 1929)

Dear Dad,

Aged nine you were taken from your home city and deposited at the Barnardo's home in Clapham.

You say you absconded from Liverpool Sheltering Home once, possibly more, and were sent away from Liverpool so you didn't have anywhere to run to. It's impossible to be sure about the rationale behind re-locating you – the copy of your record book is redacted between 21 December 1926 and 31 May 1928 – but your child's eye view of events carries a ring of truth. It seems children who were difficult were often transferred from home to home within the Barnardo's system.

The Clapham home was a way-station. Two weeks later, on 7 May 1928, you were moved on again, this time to the Barnardo's home in Hove.

You stayed in Hove for sixteen months. Did you even know you were there? You never mentioned the place.

You remembered an orphanage in Southport but that can't be right. Bardardo's records show you lived in five different Doctor Barnardo's homes, but none were located in Southport – and as far as I can tell Barnardo's didn't even have a Southport home during the time you were in their care.

Sorry, Dad, but either you forgot you were in Hove or, more likely, you were never told. It's down to those Victorian values of 'seen, not heard' children. Children were expected to be silently obedient, voiceless; question-less.

I surmise you were plucked from Liverpool Sheltering Home out of the blue and transplanted in Hove (via Clapham) without anyone explaining where you were. I think you filled the gap with Southport because it was the nearest seaside resort to your family home, possibly the only one you knew. That is my way of squaring the circle.

C

Dear Dad,

Of all the Barnardo's homes you lived in the Hove home is perhaps the most elusive.

For the other homes, Barnardo's Family History Service provided copies of old photographs and a contemporaneous newsletter (or similar) – but nothing for the Hove home. There is little information about it online. There even seems to be some confusion or lack of consistency about the home's name. Your record book shows it as the Seaside Home for Invalid Children, Hove and also Holland Road, Hove, while the cover letter from the Family History Service calls it Holland House. That led me down a blind alley for a while, as Holland House was actually a private boys' school completely unrelated to Barnardo's.

I finally stumbled across a brief description on thechildrenshome.org.uk website. The Holland Road Convalescent Home, at 65 Holland Road, Hove, was opened by Barnardo's in 1907 with accommodation for twenty boys up to the age of fifteen. It closed in 1938 and the building is now a community centre.

That's it, the sum total of my knowledge about the Hove home wrapped up in two short sentences. The fact the Hove home was a convalescent home might indicate the Superintendent of Liverpool Sheltering Home was motivated by more than getting rid of a trouble-maker; he might have been considering your status as a delicate boy,

Dad, I went there.

Your former home is a three-storey-plus-basement double-fronted yellow-brick building, smaller than Liverpool Sheltering Home and less obviously institutional, more like a grand town-house. To the rear is a small car park that possibly would once have served as the playground. The white portico over the front door is engraved with: YOUNG WOMEN'S CHRISTIAN ASSOCIATION. Presumably the YWCA took over the building sometime after Barnardo's shut the home. Holland Road Baptist Church has its office here now; the church itself is next door.

Holland Road is one of a series of avenues and roads running at right angles from Hove Lawns, a green space right next to the seafront. Some are numbered numerically from First Avenue to Fourth Avenue, with Grand Avenue in-between Second and Third, a nod to former glories. The centrepiece of the scheme is Palmeira Square, which is still impressive, although the roads flanking it lack some of their former gloss.

Hove today, like so many other Victorian-era seaside resorts, Southport included, displays a strange mix of grandeur and seediness. Its wide boulevards are more likely to house an 8 'til late shop now than a private members' club and its grand villas have mostly been converted into flats or offices.

You might not have realised at the time but your old home is in a lovely location, a short walk from the seafront. From the front steps you can turn and look back down to the sea. Perhaps you would have gone swimming or dipping when the weather allowed. The Victorians believed in the restorative power of sea-air and I imagine supervised walks by the sea would have been part of the home's routine, you boys walking down to the front two-by-two crocodile-fashion.

It would have been exhilarating. Hove beach is shingle, not sand, and drops steeply away into the English Channel. I was there on a reasonably calm day in May; even so waves were crashing and breaking on the cobbles, and the steep pebble-bank made for a challenging scramble out of the water after a chilly, morning dip.

Were you reasonably happy in Hove? I'd like to think so. But looking back at your record book I spot an entry that is longer than the rest. Like every other entry, it is handwritten in cramped cursive, mostly unpunctuated, filled with abbreviations and difficult to decipher. It is dated 15 June 1929.

Mat Supt Seaside Home for
Invalid Chldn Hove Brighton
states she has recd ltr
from Sister stating Mo. Mrs A Smith
24. Spurgeon St L'pool
died on June 5th
All ltrs in future to be add
Miss M Smith
140 Islington Liverpool
news has been broken to Robert

A large cross in the margin next to 140 Islington Liverpool is presumably intended to draw attention to the new mailing address. My eye, though, criss-crossed the page, jumping between the earlier lines: 'Mrs A Smith...died on June 5th' and the entry date '15 June 1929'.

It takes a moment for my brain to process the information, to catch its full import.

The year Agnes died: not 1924 or 1925 but 1929.

I've been looking in the wrong place all along.

C

Dear Dad,

You didn't tell me Agnes was alive when you were taken into care, or maybe you did and I didn't listen. When you spoke of the homes you didn't name them, they were simply 'the orphanages' and as far as I knew children were sent to orphanages only when they'd lost both their parents. That you could have been put into an orphanage while your mother was still living didn't occur to me. I see now that when you ran away from Liverpool Sheltering Home, your sole focus wasn't to escape from the home; you were trying to make it back to your family home, to your mother. It's heart-breaking.

Even when they moved you to Hove (Southport, you thought) you would have clung onto the hope that one day you would leave Barnardo's behind and return to Spurgeon Street and Agnes. When she died, that glimmer would be extinguished. Anyone would want the news to be broken with tenderness and sensitivity so you were let down gently. That isn't how you remember it. You remember being told your mother died because you were a naughty boy; that you broke her heart. You were ten years old.

I spent another evening on findmypast.com, revisiting my search of ancestry records. You might recall my original searches had yielded two potential Agnes Smiths and I'd discounted one because she was born too early and the other because she had died too late, but if your record book was right (and it's incredible to think it would be wrong) then the second Agnes would be a fit.

To make absolutely certain I ordered a copy of her death certificate from the General Registry Office. A week later I have it, and there she is, your mother, my Grandmother, Agnes Smith of 24 Spurgeon Street, widow of William Thomas Smith, died 3 June 1929 at 147a Mill Road. This is now the site of Liverpool Maternity Hospital but at the time it was Mill Road Infirmary. Cause of death is given as Septic Lobar Pneumonia. There is no mention of a broken heart caused by an errant youngest son. She was forty-nine.

I thought when I found out how Agnes died that the search would be over, mystery solved, but her death turns out to be a waypoint not the final destination. Why were you put into the Liverpool Sheltering Home in June 1926 when Agnes was alive until June 1929? What had happened to Agnes?

Finding the answer will be like trying to complete a jigsaw with missing pieces and no picture. The main protagonist is dead and I'm trying to piece together dry dates and half-forgotten conversations.

Suppose I could make that imaginative leap and untie the Gordian knot at the centre of your life. The real question is: should I? If Mum was here, she'd tell me to let sleeping dogs lie. Perhaps I should put the scrap of paper bearing 'Agnes Hughes' back in its envelope and forget about it and her. Perhaps that would be for the best. I worry I'm asking a question to which no one wants the answer.

What should I do? What would you have me do?

C

Clapham and Jersey (1929 to 1932)

Dear Dad,
Decision made. I continue.

Following the entry recording Agnes's death, your Barnardo's record is redacted once more. Possibly you tried running away again and were punished. The next visible entry is almost four months later, 28 September 1929, recording receipt of a letter from Bet, but by then you were no longer at the Hove home; on 16 September 1929 you'd been moved back to Clapham.

First time around you stayed in the Clapham home for less than a month. Your second stint wasn't much longer, lasting only four. On 21 January 1930 Bet was informed you were being transferred to the Barnardo's home in Gorey, Jersey on the advice of (the next word is hard to decipher, it looks like 'm/o' (an abbreviation of medical officer?)). Possibly the smog and smoke of London took its toll and it was thought best to move the delicate boy to healthier climes.

You arrived at Teighmore House, Jersey, on 24 January 1930, aged eleven, and remained there until May 1932, your longest time in any home. To my knowledge you never mentioned living in Jersey. I find that odd. I can understand a nine-year-old muddling up two Victorian-era seaside resorts such as Southport and Hove, but would an eleven-year-old, especially one as bright as you, not know you had left the mainland? Or if not then, when you returned aged thirteen? I can only imagine you knew but chose not to say. As with most everything to do with Dr Barnardo's, you seem to have sealed your Jersey memories in a part of your brain marked 'leave well alone', which in this case is a shame, because Jersey really is a beautiful island.

Although referred to as being at Gorey, Teighmore House was actually on La Rue d'Aval, more than half a mile away. It was opened in 1879 as a convalescent home for boys of delicate health and by 1930 it accommodated 100 boys. It didn't last for many years after you left, closing in 1938. Despite being situated a mile inland, Teighmore apparently had its own private section of beach in Grouville Bay. It sounds idyllic.

You would have arrived on Jersey by boat from Southampton, I expect. I arrived by plane. By a quirk of fate my visit coincided with the second wave of the Coronavirus pandemic and travel restrictions were in place to and from the UK for most countries. Jersey was part of a designated UK Common Travel Area though, which meant there were no restrictions on re-entry to the UK and none on entry to Jersey for anyone who'd received two vaccine shots in the UK (the double-jabbed) subject to being tested for COVID on arrival.

At least, that was the position when I booked the trip. The day before Dan and I were due to fly, Jersey changed their rules. We would now have to self-isolate until our test results came through, which might take up to twenty-four hours. As we were only staying for three nights, a third of our time on the island was effectively written off. (Less than two weeks later, the Jersey government changed the rules back again. My timing could hardly have been worse. There were only two weekends in the whole of spring/summer 2020 where self-isolation was required – and I chose one of them.)

In the end, it didn't affect us too much. Our lovely Airbnb host, Debbie, was happy to pick us up from the airport (allowed under the rules) and supplied us with basic groceries. We ordered food for delivery from a restaurant in St Helier. We got by until we received our test results (negative, thankfully).

By a strange quirk of fate, Debbie had grown up in a children's home in Bristol. Before we arrived she'd cycled the length of La Rue d'Aval, found Teighmore House, and worked out the best walking route.

The original Teighmore House buildings have been converted into flats. There is also an adjoining housing development, called Teighmore Park, which is on land that once belonged to the home. In a nod to the property's former use, at the entrance to the driveway to Teighmore House perched on a low, sandstone wall, is a statue of a seated boy reading a book. He's bare-footed, wearing a tunic, shorts and cap: the uniform of a Barnardo's boy.

As I've said, Jersey is a beautiful island. It's also a small one. Property supply is limited. Low supply and high demand pushes up prices. To keep a lid on prices, you need to increase supply or (if that's not possible) reduce or restrict demand, which is the Jersey Government's solution. To buy property on Jersey you need to qualify for entitled status. Broadly, if you weren't born on Jersey you need to have lived on Jersey for ten years continuously. If you are Jersey-born you still need to have lived on the island for ten years, although not necessarily continuously.

Even with this level of government intervention, Jersey property prices are high compared to mainland UK. A few months before our visit a flat in Tieghmore House sold for £960,000. What do you think of that, Dad? I don't need you to tell me. Even as I'm writing I can picture you puffing out your cheeks and shaking your head in disbelief.

C

Teighmore

Dear Dad,

The entry on 21 January 1930 recording your transfer to Teighmore is the last in your record book. There is nothing further apart from an APPLICATION FOR RESTORATION stamp dated 29 February 1932. Your two years on the island seem to have passed without incident or illness – but also apparently without any word from Bet.

After that first letter in June 1929 when she wrote to the Hove home to tell them that Agnes was dead, Bet wrote almost every month. Your record book shows letters in September 1929, October 1929, December 1929 and January 1930. She even raised a query over two letters and a parcel that weren't acknowledged. ('Mrs Gardner asked to make enquiries so we may tell sister.')

But once you were sent to Jersey: nothing.

Bet could have lost interest, of course, but in that case you'd expect her letters to become less frequent over time, gradually tailing off until finally stopping altogether. Possibly her letters to Teighmore simply weren't recorded. Given what followed it seems unlikely she cut ties. On 12 May 1932 you travelled from Teighmore to Barnardo's Stepney Receiving House. The next day, a little over two years after arriving on Jersey, you were 'restored to sister'. Having spent six years in four different Barnardo's homes, you were finally discharged and sent back to Liverpool to live with Bet.

The only photograph I have of you as a child is from that day, freedom day. The Barnardo's Archive Officer kindly sent it to me; it forms part of their image library. I wonder if you ever saw it? Aged thirteen and a half you're smartly dressed in jacket, shirt and tie, and in your breast pocket is a neatly folded handkerchief. You're seated, arms folded, unsmiling, looking directly into the camera.

I've spent a long time staring at that photograph, trying to read your expression. The boy in the photograph stares back, eyes slightly narrowed, enigmatic as Mona Lisa. Is he happy? Relieved? There's something about the set of his mouth, a slight curl of the lip, suggestive of scorn or superciliousness – a teenager's disdain for Doctor Barnardo's captured in black and white even as he was about to leave their homes for good.

C

Old Barn Road (1932 to 1939)

Dear Dad,

When you moved back to Liverpool you found a ready-made family waiting for you. During your two-year stint in Jersey, Bet had acquired a husband and a baby son.

You'd last seen Bet in 1926 – half your life ago – before you were put into care when she was a live-in domestic servant at Elizabeth Street. Three years later, when she registered Agnes's death and informed Dr Barnardo's, she was at an address in Islington, presumably still a live-in-domestic. Only six months later, when you were being moved to Jersey, Bet had also moved again, to 16 Lundie Street, Everton, a move that changed her life. 16 Lundie Street was the home of Charles and Ethel Gorton and through them (I expect) she met Charles's younger brother, Richard. They married that same year.

When you think about it, it was asking a lot of Bet and Richard Gorton to take you in. They were only twenty-three, had been married for less than two years and had a baby son, Reginald Richard Gorton born in October 1931, who was six months old. Six years in residential care wouldn't have prepared you for the rough and tumble of young family life. Yet they made a place for you in their home.

Richard, like Bet, was nine years your senior, a father-figure and big brother rolled into one. You became firm friends, a friendship that lasted a lifetime.

Richard and Bet not only gave you a home, they gave you a job, setting you to work in their greengrocer's shop. You were approaching school leaving age (then fourteen) and Bet needed an assistant. Finding work elsewhere would have been difficult, if not impossible. The Great Depression had hit Liverpool badly.

It would have seemed like a perfect arrangement. I picture you in a grocer's apron a few sizes too big alongside crates of apples and potatoes outside the shop, or riding through the streets on an ancient tradesman's bike piled high with customers' orders.

So the years passed as years do. For the next seven years you were part of the Gorton family, living in the family home at 2 Old Barn Road, a tiny two-up, two-down terrace not far from Liverpool Football Club, going to work each day at the family greengrocer's shop, coming home each evening to a meal cooked by Bet, looking after Reg when Bet was occupied. Aged sixteen, you became an uncle second-time over when Bet and Richard had a second child, a daughter named Thelma Dorothea, on 23 April 1935. Thelma sleeps in a cot in Bet and Richard's room; you and Reg share the other bedroom.

Like the Gorton family the city of Liverpool was also growing, with the population reaching its peak level of 855,000, almost double what it is today. As a result the construction industry was booming creating much-needed jobs, not only in housing but in commercial and civic projects. Palace Ice Rink opened in 1931, Liverpool Boxing Stadium and Ritz Roller Rink in 1932, Seaforth Greyhound Stadium in 1933. Speke Airport opened in 1933; the East Lancashire Road and the Mersey Queensway Tunnel both opened the following year. The city was building its future.

New cinemas with exotic-sounding names were popping up like daffodils in Spring – Commodore, Astoria, Paramount, Reo, Tatler, Majestic, Plaza; not altogether surprising when cinema attendances in the city were estimated at a staggering 576,000 per week. Football pools took off around the same time. Vernons's headquarters opened in Liverpool in 1934, the first purpose-built offices constructed by a UK pools company. Four years later, Littlewoods Pools's iconic building opened on Edge Lane

Above all there was the beautiful game. Football ruled the city's heart and mind, then as now. In the 1930s the Blues wore the crown. Everton won the 1932 FA Cup Final, beating Manchester City 3-0 with goals scored by Jimmy Stein, Dixie Dean and James Dunn.

Where you part of any of this? I know you weren't among the crowds thronging the entrance of the Queensway tunnel trying to catch a glimpse of King George V at the official opening; you said you were working. But you might have joined the crowds lured to the Picture Houses or the sports stadia. Did you laugh at the Three Stooges in *Disorder in Court* and root for James Cagney in *Angels with Dirty Faces?* Did you cheer in disbelief as Liverpool slotted six past Everton at Anfield without reply, watch in horror as local favourite Nel Tarleton narrowly missed out on the world featherweight title, losing on points to America's Freddie Miller; even attend your first baseball game, a World Cup match between England and the USA held in Wavertree Gardens?

You told me nothing about those years. All your stories came from before or after. I only remember you saying you worked long hours for pocket money, that you were Bet's skivvy in effect. Or perhaps it was Mum who said that. But more than the hard work and low pay, it irked you that Bet could not or would not answer the question that still kept you awake at night.

Bet claimed to know nothing about why you were sent to Liverpool Sheltering Home all those years ago. She refused to talk about it, or about Agnes. Perhaps she thought it was the best thing to do. Least said, soonest mended, isn't that what Mum would have said? For you, though, avoiding the subject worsened the pain of not knowing and took on a life of its own. Whenever you and Bet were alone in the shop or at home, it would be there too, until eventually it seemed as if 2 Old Barn Road contained six residents: Richard, Bet, Reg, Thelma, you and Not-Talking-About-It.

After seven years at Old Barn Road and the greengrocer's shop, your living and working arrangements had started to seem not so perfect after all.

C

Dear Dad,

1939. The ill-wind whipping through the Gorton family home was nothing compared to the black clouds gathering over Europe and beyond. A storm is approaching. Germany had annexed Austria, Czechoslovakia and Lithuania, and begun its pogrom against Jewish citizens; Italy had invaded Albania. In spite of Mr Chamberlain's piece of paper, there will not be peace in your time. History blows in, flattens everything in its path and sweeps you up.

A few weeks after 3 September 1939 when Britain declared war on Germany, the British Government organised a National Register to gather information about the civilian population. They needed this to issue identity cards and ration books and organise conscription. By the end of September 1939 the personal details of about forty million individuals had been recorded. I'm interested in five of them.

Richard, Bet and four-year old Thelma were still at 2 Old Barn Road.

Reg, aged seven, was in Aberystwyth, evacuated from Liverpool and sent to Cardiganshire to board with a family called Evans.

And you? You're not listed.

I couldn't understand it. I searched and searched and searched again.

Then I realised there was a very simple explanation. Lord Kitchener might have put you in a home but Neville Chamberlain didn't put you in the army.

I'd always taken it as read that you'd been conscripted but your name isn't on the National Register because you weren't a civilian in September 1939. Months before Chamberlain tore up his futile Peace Pact and pushed conscription legislation through Parliament, you had jumped into the arms of a recruiting sergeant and enlisted; while the government was still information-gathering you were billeted in a military training camp, aged twenty, preparing to go to war.

Why didn't you tell me?

C

War (1939 to 1945)

Enlisted at DSR 3-9-39 Wimbledon
TA   4   Royal Artillery   24 APR 1939
Age (in years) on enlistment   20
Trade on enlistment   Greengrocer
Religion   C/E

No. Of Part II Order or other Authority	Unit		Army Rank	Dates
34/39	226/57 A/T	Attested & Posted	GNR	24.4.39
1/39		Attended Annual Camp for 15 (days) 1939		2.6.39
		EMBODIED under 13 (2) (b) TA Regulations 1936		1.9 39
6/40	50th A/T	Training Regt RA Posted	Gnr	22.12.39
32/40 244	61st A/T	Regt Posted	"	13.4.40

Extract from military service file Army No 1455413 New No 22208092
Robert Smith

Dear Dad,

You told me very little about your war-time service and I never asked. I wish I'd been more curious as a child; I guess I'm trying to make up for that now.

I gained access to your service file from the Ministry of Defence. I hope you don't mind.

On 24 April 1939 you enlisted into the Territorial Army. On that date you ceased to be plain Mister Smith, Greengrocer; at a pen-stroke you were transformed into Gunner Smith of the 226th Anti-Tank Battery of the 57th Anti-Tank Regiment of the Royal Regiment of Artillery (CDAA branch).

(You signed the enlistment papers in Wimbledon, for the Surrey TA, although you give a Liverpool address: 1 Croft Road (can't read next two words) Anfield. When did you move out of Old Barn Road? Were you living over the greengrocer's shop? And how did you come to be in Wimbledon?)

I used to think of the Territorial Army as overgrown boys playing games, an adult version of the Scouts or the Duke of Edinburgh Awards. I've realised only recently that members of the TA agree to be called up for full military service when needed. When you joined the TA this is what you signed up to do.

You must have known it would only be a matter of time. It was clear which way the wind was blowing.

The call-up came four months later on 2 September 1939. Hitler had invaded Poland the day before; the next day Britain was at war.

C

Dear Dad,

I can't settle on why you decided to join-up, knowing you'd be first to be called-up to fight.

Did you want some adventure in your life, a chance to travel and see the world? You were at that age.

Was it your sense of duty, the belief that fighting Fascism was the right thing to do?

Did you decide to jump before you were pushed, while you could still choose the corps, the role?

Perhaps you simply wanted something, anything to happen. After seven years with Bet, Richard, and their two children, living with them, working in their greengrocers shop, I imagine you were wondering: is this it? Life was out there somewhere, passing you by. As strange as it sounds, perhaps you joined the army because you wanted to live.

Did Bet try to talk you out of joining up? Did she pressure Richard into getting you a job at the foundry where he worked? Foundry workers were key workers and Richard's job, press tool setter, was a reserved occupation, one of the key jobs that it was in the national interest to protect, which is why he remained at home throughout the war. This would have been clear to all of you; the Minister of Labour had presented a provisional Schedule of Reserved Occupations to Parliament as early as January 1939.

The job you took a decade later, iron moulder, was a reserved occupation too. Richard put a word in for you in the late 1940s so why not in January 1939 when, Chamberlain's Peace Pact notwithstanding, Britain was already gearing up for a possible war against Nazi Germany?

There's something else I've only now learned from reading the notes to the Schedule. As well as being exempt from conscription men in reserved occupations were prohibited from enlisting for war-time service, and nor could they volunteer in peace–time for part-time service in a role that would become full-time in war. They'd be barred from joining the TA, for example.

It would only be natural for Bet to want to protect her little brother. She was a forceful lady. I can imagine her giving Richard no peace until he'd lined you up a job at the foundry. Is that why you signed up in Wimbledon? You bolted before Bet could close the stable door.

C

Dear Dad,

It was June 1939. You were sent to an annual camp for fifteen days' training.

There was PT in the gym, marching, fieldwork, lectures, rifle-shooting, getting to know the weight and feel of a 303 Lee-Enfield or a Tommy Gun. You were taught how to dig a slit trench and crawl in wet grass. Once or twice there was night training, killing time playing card games, waiting for the sun to set.

Saturday morning saw everyone on parade in the large parade ground. Anybody not properly dressed or making a mistake would be given a day's potato peeling at the cookhouse or made to wash dirty dishes for two hours or more after duty.

On the last day there was more rifle shooting, thirty men in a troop with an instructor and sergeant. The sergeant took bets on who would get the highest score, one shilling each. At the end he called out his own score as the highest and pocketed the cash, though none of the men had seen his target. You didn't mind; you got what you came for: the rank of gunner on your record.

Only a few months later you were called up to full service, posted to the 50th Anti-Tank Regiment.

Attending the annual camp had given you a taste of army life. Full service was better, if anything, as you received full army pay, 17s. 6d. per week. You could easily manage on that, living full-time at the camp. A cup of tea cost tuppence, ten cigarettes tuppence ha'penny, a meal out one shilling and sixpence – you didn't need much else. Some men went to the pictures in their evenings off (cost one shilling) but you were never one for the movies.

You trained every day except Sundays. You were taught to fire Howitzers, 100 lb shell guns made for trench warfare in World War One, the names of battles scratched onto them like scars: Mons, Ypres, Passchendaele, Verdun. Some days there were route marches, thirty miles with full kit, rifle and all, weighing 30 lbs. Afterwards the doctor ordered light duties, serving drinks and snacks in the Sergeants' Mess, to allow time for blisters to heal.

On your free Sundays you sometimes went back to Old Barn Road. Bet would keep you waiting on the doorstep a little longer than necessary before answering the door. She'd want the neighbours to get a good look at her young brother in his uniform. Even for a family visit you'd not be allowed to leave the camp unless you were fully kitted out: khaki shirt tucked into khaki trousers, trousers neatly belted and tucked into anklets, boots polished to a shine, cap bearing the distinctive badge of the Royal Artillery: a muzzle-loading gun sandwiched between a crown and the single word 'Ubique' (Everywhere), and the scrolled motto 'Quo Fas et Gloria Ducant' (Wherever Right and Glory Lead).

You were moved around, posted to other regiments within the RA, to other camps. At some point you were stationed back in Wimbledon. Here, among Southerners, your vowels shifted. 'Bath' and 'scone' began rhyming with 'hearth' and 'cone' instead of the usual Northern "math" and "gone".

In April 1940 you were posted to the 266th Battery of the 61st Anti-Tank Regiment. You had your first regimental guard duty, a twenty-four-hour shift, two hours on and four hours off. Walking around the huts at midnight you saw someone coming and, heart pounding, yelled 'Who goes there?', but the 'stranger' was only the duty officer, checking you were being alert.

Spare time was spent playing cards or other games. Anything can become a game if you put your mind to it. Put a stick or a knife in the ground and draw a line about nine feet away, stand behind the line, throw coins at the stick, nearest coin wins. And when everyone grew bored with games there'd be sing-a-longs to pass time, 'We're the Boys of the Royal Artillery' or songs from the First World War: 'It's a Long Way to Tipperary', 'Pack Up Your Troubles', 'Mademoiselle from Armentieres'.

Not that there was much spare time anymore. You were now training for two to three weeks at a time on and off base, climbing up nets, crawling under nets, firing STEN guns to range, climbing up ropes, throwing live hand grenades. You only had five seconds after pulling the pin so you learned to move fast.

You camped out. Sometimes there were tents, sometimes not; then you slept under tarpaulin on a line, pulled tight over your head to stay dry if it was raining hard.

Inspections continued as before even after three weeks' wild camping. Anyone not properly dressed or unshaven would be in for seven days' cookhouse duties.

That's how I imagine it, anyway, your day to day life in the army. The truth is I know nothing, not even where your camp was located.

C

Dear Dad,

Bit by bit, I'm slowly gathering facts and weaving them together to create a story, but I won't know for sure if the story works until I'm nearing the end and find pieces that don't fit. Even if I manage to bind everything into one cohesive narrative, how fairly it mirrors the truth only you will know. About your early life in the army you told me Zero, Zilch, Nothing, De Nada...

What did you do, exactly, how did you spend your days, during those three years and thirty-five days on home service? Did my previous letter hit the mark?

I wrote the truth. That is, those things did happen but not necessarily to you. They were memories recorded in a BBC archive by Brail99, who was a gunner from 1942 to 1946. How else can I get a feel for what your life was like back then? All I know for sure is that you were a gunner in the Royal Artillery and in May 1942 you were called into action.

By then Germany had invaded Denmark, Norway, Holland, Belgium, France, Greece, Yugoslavia, Russia and North Africa, and was blitzing Britain and Malta. The future was looking very bleak.

C

Military History Sheet
Services at home and abroad

Country	Service to count as British or Indian	From	To	Years	Days
HOME		24.4.39	31.8.39		130
HOME Emb	BRITISH	1.9.39	26.5.42	2	268
MEF	"	27.5.42	10.7.44	2	45

Medals and Decorations, Clasps and Annuities
Awarded the Africa Star, 8th Army Clasp

Extract from military service file Army No 1455413 New No 22208092

Robert Smith

Dear Dad,

The Royal Regiment of the Artillery (usually known simply as the Royal Artillery) was the largest regiment in the British Army. It was made up of different types of regiment, variously responsible for providing field, medium, heavy, super heavy, anti-tank and anti-aircraft units.

You were in an anti-tank unit.

Those are the dry facts, so dry you could take a match to them. Where could I begin to find a way into the story?

As it turned out, with something you always regretted losing, your war medals, in particular the Africa Star with the Eighth Army Clasp.

The breakthrough came by accident, the result of an idle evening browsing Liverpool Central Library's online catalogue. It turns out you were part of something incredible.

The Eighth Army fought its way across North Africa from Egypt to Tunisia, then via Sicily across the whole of mainland Italy from the toe to the foothills of the Alps.

It was pitched against General Rommel (the famous Desert Fox) and his superior panzer battle tanks. It was commanded by General Sir Bernard Montgomery, who made such a name for himself he was known simply as Monty. It included the 7th Armoured Division (the famous Desert Rats).

It fought across deserts and mountains. It marched further and battled for longer than any other army in the Second World War

So: fighting against the odds, travelling huge distances, adapting to extremes of terrain...but there is more.

The Eighth Army was a uniquely cosmopolitan force, a British army that included soldiers from Australia, Canada, New Zealand, South Africa, India, Nepal, France, Greece, Poland and more besides. If a single army could be said to symbolise the World's fight against fascism, it was the Eighth.

Dad, why did you never tell me?
C

Dear Dad,

North Africa: a campaign born from the need to protect the Suez Canal.

They say attack is the best form of defence; accordingly troops were sent from Egypt (technically independent but de facto controlled by Britain) across the border into Libya (an Italian colony) the day after Italy entered the Second World War in June 1940.

Things went one way then the other until Tubrok, which the British had captured, was under siege. By the time you arrived in May 1942, the Eighth Army had already crossed into Libya – November 1941, the first time they were in action as an army – to attack Rommel's Panzerarmee Afrika and relieve Tubrok.

Your first taste of action, the month-long Battle of Gazala, didn't go well. Despite superior numbers of men and tanks the Eighth Army (then under General Auchinleck) was tactically out-thought and forced into a chaotic retreat into Egypt. It would be a year and a change of general before Rommel was defeated at the Battle of El Alamein, and the Eighth could begin pursuing the Axis armies across Libya, reaching the Tunisian border in February 1943.

You were in the area of the Sahara known as the Western Desert for a year. It would be a hard place to live, let alone fight.

Sand can be a nuisance even in temperate UK. I love living in a seaside town but when it's windy, which it often is, the sand kicks up, encroaching onto the promenade and the roads beyond, blocking drains, drifting into roof-spaces, gradually filling up eaves. Sand is invading my town, silently; it threatens the town's future, we're told. The beach has risen by a metre in ten years. Sand acts slowly but steadily. It has time on its side.

So I close my eyes and imagine living for a year in a place where there is nothing but sand, dust and sand, sand and dust, as far as the eye can see.

Sand acted as saboteur in the Desert campaign. It flayed and blinded in violent dust storms. It jammed the workings of vehicles, tanks, guns, and radio equipment, rendering them useless. It got into bed rolls and clothing, rubbing at soft skin, causing deep suppurating ulcers, desert sores. It snuck into food. You would have slept in sand, eaten sand, and breathed sand.

There was also sickness, mainly dysentery and jaundice, and gun-shot wounds, some self-inflicted. Water was short, of course, and fresh food was rare. In summer the heat was almost too much to bear but in winter nights were often freezing. Blankets were in short supply.

When you were there it would have been especially hard. In the winter of 1942/43 the rains came, torrential rains that turned the desert into a swamp and covered everything in a blanket of fog.

Despite all the hardships and privations I expect there were moments of wonder, too: the changing colours and forms of the desert, endless variations of low ridges and soft sand, a landscape continually reshaping and shifting, sometimes overnight, sometimes before your eyes, the sun going down over mile after mile of salt flat; a sense of remoteness in the hubbub of war.

Most of all, Dad, I like to imagine you singing the German love song adopted by all the desert armies, British, German and Italian: 'Lili Marlene'.

The Eighth captured Tripoli in January 1943 then advanced into Tunisia, meeting up with Anglo-American forces advancing from the west and fighting alongside them until May 1943 when the Axis forces surrendered.

One year after you landed in North Africa and two thousand miles from El Alamein, the Eighth had finally achieved its goal. Axis forces had withdrawn, the war in North Africa was over, and you were awarded your first medal.

It was a six-pointed star. The central inscription GRI VI was surrounded by a circlet inscribed THE AFRICA STAR and surmounted by a crown. I know this from pictures. Your medal was lost. I never saw it or held it in my palm, cold metal against skin, admiring the weight and the feel of it; you never had the chance to show it off to me, or explain that the shiny yellow metal was not gold but a copper zinc alloy, and the central design was the Royal Cipher of King George VI.

Did you ever meet Monty? I read he always led from the front and made himself visible to the ordinary soldiers.

Did you parade in front of Churchill in Tripoli, when he visited to celebrate that city's fall?

Was North Africa your first contact with American soldiers? I expect you weren't impressed. By all accounts the Americans drank the local wine as if it was beer and the gutters of Tripoli were filled with drunken GI Joes.

Beer, wine, whatever was drunk, in whatever quantities, they – and you – had earned it. But your war was not over. There was a lot more fighting to come.

C

Dear Dad

Victory in North Africa was a prelude to the Italian campaign, which began with the invasion of Sicily in July 1943.

Sicily presented new challenges: roads designed for donkey-and-cart transport were not easily navigable by tanks and supply trucks; hill-towns and mountain villages were ideal for defence but hard to attack; and mosquitoes, deadly malarial mosquitoes. The latter was the hardest to overcome.

I've returned from enough holidays covered in red, itchy wheals to know first-hand how perfectly adapted is the female mosquito to feeding on human blood. Did you know it is only the female that bites?

She is so light you do not feel her land. Her proboscis has the strength to piece skin but is so fine you do not feel her injecting the anticoagulant that prevents your blood clotting as she sucks. You will know her by sound only, an unmistakable whine as she flies past your ear. By then it is usually too late, she has already fed and if you manage to swat her it will be your blood, not hers, spattered against the wall.

She is a tiny winged syringe, moving from person to person, biting and feeding until she is full. Sometimes she is loaded with the malaria parasite, potentially infecting whoever she bites with a deadly disease. One bite is all it might take.

That was how it was in Sicily in 1943. All soldiers were issued with mosquito repellent cream (although some swore the cream attracted the mosquitoes), and ordered to take a daily mepacrine tablet and wear rolled-down sleeves and long trousers after dusk. Still the mosquitoes bit. For the female mosquitoes of Sicily, the invading soldiers were an all-you-can-eat buffet.

Once injected, the malaria parasite moves through the blood to the liver where it multiplies; from there into red blood cells, which burst, releasing more parasites. The body fights this invasion with fever: high temperatures, sweats, chills, loss of appetite, muscle pains; also diarrhoea, vomiting, difficulty breathing, headaches, dizziness, and fainting. In Sicily during July and August 1943 more men were put out of action by malaria than by mines, bullets and shells.

You ran the gauntlet of dirt roads, marsh, thick undergrowth, and voracious mosquitoes – and enemy soldiers, of course – but thankfully only for a couple of months. At the end of August, German forces withdrew and suddenly you were in mainland Italy.

C

Dear Dad,

Eighth Army landed in the toe of mainland Italy in September 1943, linking up with the US Fifth Army. Some of Eighth Army were sent to serve with the US Fifth and the two armies were tasked with fighting their way into Central Italy and Rome.

You arrived on the cusp of autumn, harbouring a memory of pre-war posters of 'sunny Italy', believing Italian soldiers were as likely to run or surrender as to dig in and fight.

You were in for a shock on both counts. Italy may be hot in summer but autumn and winter bring rain and snow; and now the Italians were on home soil, defending their country against invasion, they showed more grit than they ever had in the Western Desert. And, as before, you were also up against the drilled and disciplined German army.

The Italians and Germans had geography on their side. The Appenines, running down Italy's spine and splitting the country in two, was an excellent position for the Axis Armies' defensive artillery and an obstacle for the attacking Allies. But an even bigger obstacle to progress was the weather.

Autumn/winter 1943: rain fell relentlessly day after day. Rivers, swollen with rain, flooded the plains; the ground became a quagmire, impossible for troops and tanks to move across. Men were soaked to the skin, plastered with mud, and bitterly cold. Autumn/winter 1944, having pressed further north, was even worse. Mountains were covered in snow; it was freezing cold and foggy.

The wet and cold took its toll. Men were put out of action with trench-foot, respiratory problems, hepatitis, jaundice – as many as were killed or wounded in battle.

The Eighth also had to contend with strategic losses. Australian units were redeployed to fight the Japanese; other units were sent to France. Even their beloved Monty was recalled home to help plan the Normandy landings.

It was hard to take, particularly as the Italian campaign was far from over. Fighting was fierce and gunners were kept busy; the artillery guns demanded it. You would have dug gun pits, cleaned guns, unloaded ammo when the truck came round; it was never enough, the guns always required more. You ate on the hoof, running to the kitchen and bringing back your meal to eat at the gun, washing and shaving only when you could fit it in; grabbing a couple of hours sleep whenever the guns could spare you. The guns were your taskmasters, your tyrants, your guardian angels; you needed each other.

The US Fifth entered Rome in June 1944.

The fall of Rome was hugely symbolic for the Allied Armies – but the very next day, 6 June 1944, the Normandy landings took place. Newspapers and newsreels turned their spotlight on France, France, France; Italy was dropped like a bomb.

As you continued advancing towards Florence, then onwards through Northeast Italy towards the Austrian border, you might have received a letter from Bet assuming fighting had finished in Italy. What were you doing there? Would you soon be back in action in France? Eighth Army soldiers received many such letters from loved ones at home.

Word spread among the men that an MP, Lady Astor, had called them D-Day Dodgers (even though D-Day means the start of any military operation, and the Eighth had endured many D-Days). Lady A denied it but it was too late, the rumour had already taken hold.

Your sacrifices were being ignored and – worse – denied. It must have felt as if the nation had dumped you in a nightmare then turned its back.

With typical British black-humour, the Eighth resurrected their favourite desert anthem, 'Lili Marlene', with new, sarcastic lyrics, no longer singing about a remembered sweetheart but about how easy life supposedly was for you in Italy, drinking wine and partying in Rome with the Yanks, landing in Salerno to cheers and free beer from Jerry, taking a bus to Florence and swimming in the Po, and generally having a lovely time in the sunshine: a holiday on full pay!

Did you feel bitter?

You hadn't been home for years. You had seen so much destruction and horror; known friends who would be left behind in Italy forever. And still the fighting continued, uphill, across swollen rivers and ground sown with mines and booby traps, doggedly pushing north.

I imagine you were tired, deeply, deeply tired.
C

No. Of Part II Order or other Authority	Unit		Army Rank	Dates
2317/44	84 A/T	Trans, to Infantry (London Scottish)	"	2.7.44

Military History Sheet

Services at home and abroad

Country	Service to count as British or Indian	From	To	Years	Days
BNAF		11.9.44	5.1.46	1	179

Wounded

Wounded 22.12.44

Extract from military service file Army No 1455413 New No 22208092

Robert Smith

Dear Dad,

I was almost thirty before I learned you'd fought in Italy.

I was planning to visit Lake Como. You told me you were near Lake Como when Mussolini was captured and shot. You told me the Italian people crowded the streets to cheer the Allied soldiers and an Italian woman gave you ice-cream; you said you felt like a hero.

It was the only time you talked to me directly about what you did during the war.

Of course, I knew you'd fought. Your claw hand was evidence, a permanent reminder of the bullet you took to the inside of your forearm a year into the Italian campaign, from American friendly fire. (It was 22 December 1944. The field hospital removed the bullet but botched the repair and damaged your flexor muscle, or perhaps the muscle was irreparably damaged by the bullet. Maybe it was simply that there was no aftercare – there's no time for physiotherapy when you're fighting a war.)

So, too, was the way you spoke. You served with the London Scottish Regiment for less than a year but it was long enough to embed Scottish dialect words into your everyday vocabulary: och aye, nesh, blether.

But you were naturally taciturn and what-did-you-do-in-the-war-Dad was not on my conversational radar.

Writing this I remember a conversation we had when I was a teenager.

It was the mid-eighties, there was apartheid in South Africa and the hot topic of the day was whether or not the UK should impose sanctions. I was adamant that if anti-apartheid activists, including much-respected Bishop Desmond Tutu, advocated sanctions, we should do it. You said we should never interfere in other people's countries. Like most young people, I saw the world in black and white and thought I knew it all. I sneered about how you'd fought in World War Two, therefore had massively interfered in other people's countries – duh! You shrugged. I thought I'd won the argument. I didn't understand I was looking at it the wrong way around, viewing history in reverse.

I find myself worrying over that conversation as a dog might worry a sheep. It was an insult to label your actions in World War Two as interference, to reduce everything you'd fought for to that level. The UK responded to the invasion of Poland, we weren't the aggressors. If you'd tried to explain, would I have listened? No, probably not and you knew it, hence that shrug. I wish you'd tried, though, at least tried to make me understand what motivated you, aged twenty, to enlist in the army when war was looming; why you chose to put yourself in danger rather than sit out the war at home under the shelter of an occupational exemption. The fact we never had that chat left us both the poorer.

The citizens of Italy were right, you were a hero. I never told you that before but why would I? I'm only now beginning to understand.
C

Peace (1945 to 1953)

Part II/III Order No and Date	Unit	Personal Occurrence	Rank	Date
Y List CMF 87/45	RASC	Transferred	DVR	7.6.45
CMF 1445/45	72CY	Emb CMF for leave in UK LLAP	DVR	20.7.45
53/45	65TC	Disemb UK for 28 days leave [LLAP]	DVR	30.7.45
162/45	"	Embarked UK for o/s CTBA	DVR	29.8.45
6552	GHQ 2 ECH CMF	Detrained at Milan, Completed 28 days leave		1.9.45

Extract from military service file Army No 1455413 New No 22208092
Robert Smith

Dear Dad,

By April 1945 the Allies were breaking through the last German defences in northern Italy and Italian citizens were rising up against the Fascist regime.

Mussolini fled Milan and headed north in an attempt to escape across the border into Switzerland with his mistress. They were captured on 27 April by partisans near Dongo on Lake Como. The next day they were driven to the village of Giulino di Mezzegra on Lake Como and executed by machine gun fire. Their bodies were taken to Milan and dumped in a square, where they were beaten by an angry mob and hung upside down from a girder.

Two days later, Hitler committed suicide. Germany surrendered a week afterwards on 8 May 1945.

It was over. World War Two – in Europe – had come to an end.

Most Eighth Army soldiers began counting down the days to their return home. Not you, though; you wanted to stay.

Why stay on?

I can see how the army would have given you a feeling of belonging, possibly for the first time in your life. In the army, everyone works together for the same cause; I imagine you weren't ready to let go of that camaraderie. Also what was there for you back home? You would see yourself moving back in with Bet, Richard and the children, back in your old job in the grocer's shop or something similar. You were twenty-six, almost a quarter of your life spent in the army, at war or preparing for war. In comparison, your old life in Liverpool would have seemed dull, dull, dull.

By the time Eighth Army soldiers began making their journeys home in July, you had already made your decision. In June 1945 you had signed up for another three years of army life, enlisting into the Royal Army Service Corps as a driver.

Looking back, I was remarkably incurious about what that involved. You told me you sometimes drove officers around but I never asked who they were, where they went, the type of vehicle or what you did the rest of the time, when there were no officers to be driven. It wouldn't simply be hopping into a vehicle and a straightforward drive from A to B. As a driver you'd be responsible for repairing and maintaining your vehicle and with roads destroyed or impassable it would likely involve some off-road skills.

RASC transported all manner of supplies: food, water, fuel, clothing and other general domestic stores, such as stationery and furniture. It was logistically impossible to repatriate all servicemen immediately after VE Day and while they remained in a camp they needed food, drink, cigarettes.

Specialist troops were needed to clear landmines and defuse unexploded bombs, repair roads, bridges, power cables, telephone lines, and water supplies, and re-open ports and waterways blocked by sunken vessels and anti-invasion obstacles. Others were needed to deal with the human wreckage of displaced persons, including millions of refugees and released POWs. They, too, needed supplies, needed a man like you, an enabler, someone to help them turn chaos into order.

You could say you played a part in putting post-war Europe back together again.

Why am I doing this, writing letters to you about your own life? I set out with a clear aim of finding Agnes but two years and many letters later the investigation seems to have taken on a life of its own and morphed into something else.

Am I still trying to solve the mystery of what happened to Agnes and why you became a Barnardo's boy? Or am I really trying to understand why we stopped talking?
C

Country	Service to count as British or Indian	From	To	Years	Days
HOME		6.1.46	16.4.46		101
Class Z (T) Res		17.4.46	4.7.48	2	79

Part II/III Order No and Date	Personal Occurrence	Rank	Date
	Disembarked Hastings	DVR	6.1.46
	Proceeded on release leave		7.1.46
	RELEASED to CLASS 'Z' (T) ROYAL ARMY RESERVE	DVR	17.4.46
	Disch'd Para 204 (6) TA Regs. His services being no longer requ'd on re-enlistment on a Reg Army S/S engagement	DVR	4.7.48

Extract from military service file Army No 1455413 New No 22208092
Robert Smith

Dear Dad,

By the beginning of 1946, your work for the army was effectively over. They had nothing left for you to do. They supplied you with suit, shirt, tie, and overcoat, the usual civvies, and released you to Class Z Reserve, a contingent consisting of soldiers who had served since 3 September 1939 who were liable to recall if needed.

One day you were a driver in the RASC; the next you had no job and no place to call home – apart from Old Barn Road; so you headed back to Liverpool.

Were you shocked at what you found when you returned?

Liverpool in 1946 was a very different city to the one you left only four years previously.

The city's docks were vital to the Trans-Atlantic shipping route, bringing essential supplies into the country, and during the war the basement of Exchange Chambers had been transformed into the command centre for the entire Allied War in the Atlantic. In May 1941, a year before you set sail for North Africa, the skies over Liverpool began raining bombs. The Luftwaffe had no trouble locating the target; despite strict blackouts, on a clear moon-lit night the River Mersey, seen from the sky, was a broad, silver finger pointing right at the heart of the city.

The pounding continued for seven nights. Landmark buildings such as the old Customs House were destroyed outright or demolished due to bomb damage. Nor was the devastation confined to the city centre. Liverpool's dock network extended seven miles from Brunswick to Seaforth on the east side of the Mersey and from Birkenhead to Wallasey on the west side. Swathes of houses were destroyed towards the north of the city, your old stomping ground. People emerged from bomb shelters to find whole roads had disappeared overnight, the entire streetscape changed, gone.

Then, inexplicably, it stopped.

If the Blitz had gone on much longer, Liverpool might have been bombed into oblivion, razed to the ground, wiped off the map, but the Pier Head survived, the Liver Building survived, the Town Hall survived, St George's Hall survived, the Albert Dock survived, morale survived; Liverpool survived.

If ever I meet someone visiting the city, I suggest they stop by the bombed out church of St Luke. I tell them the church took a direct hit in the May Blitz, an incendiary bomb dropping straight through its roof, engulfing it in fire and destroying everything inside, even the stain glass windows, which popped and shattered in the heat; the building itself, though, stood firm and the stone shell still stands, a living war memorial. I explain the depth of affection us locals feel for this church-shell, how we've resisted all attempts to demolish it; that open-air concerts and food-and-drink festivals are held there in summer and the former churchyard is now a landscaped Peace Garden, a pleasant place to sit on a sunny day amid the hurly-burly of the city.

If they're still listening, I try to make them understand how our affection for the bombed out church says something about Scousers, something more than the usual stuff about our love of football and music and our sense of humour, something more personal and profound. The shell of St Luke's church symbolises Liverpool's survival against all the odds. It is refusing to be beaten-down by adversity; it is defiance; it is resistance. Above all, it is heart. I've always been proud to call Liverpool my city; I'll never understand why you claim to hate it.

But this is now. Back in 1946, Dad, you returned to a city where 2500 explosives had been dropped less than five years previously, making it the most bombed city in the UK outside London. War had transformed its landscape.

I expect you hardly recognised the place.

C

Dear Dad,

I imagine it was through Richard Gorton that you got work in a wire works then an iron moulding business.

By April 1946 most available blue-collar jobs would have gone, taken by men already de-mobbed. Richard would have put in a good word, given you an in with his employer. It was the least he could do having sat out the war at home, safe in his protected occupation as a press tool setter – an occupation (like wire, like iron moulding) associated with foundries.

I never asked you what an iron moulder was, what you did, exactly, or where you worked. I've since learned that an iron moulder made the moulds that were used to fashion metal castings. You would have done this by hand-pressing sand into special moulding flasks. Each moulder had an individual identification tag which they used to mark their completed moulds. It was a skilled trade.

Harland & Wolff, the shipbuilders famous for building the Titanic, had a foundry in Strand Road, Bootle, so my guess is you worked there. I imagine there would be a certain satisfaction in iron moulding: working with moist sand, judging the exact volume and compression needed to create the perfect mould, visualising the countries people will travel to because of the ship part you're helping to shape: America, Canada, Australia, New Zealand, South Africa.

Much like the army, iron moulding was a team effort. By the 1940s castings were generally mass produced, but men were still needed at every stage of the process: loading sand into the sand storage bins, placing weights on the moulds as they passed into the pouring room, filling the ladles, removing weights from the cooled moulds, tying the castings into bundles ready for shipment. I'd like to think you were, if not happy, then at least content in your work.

But the late 1940s was a bad time to work in the iron and steel industry. For almost a decade business had been buoyed by the government rearming for war and by the war itself. Peacetime brought a drop in demand. It was Boom then Bust.

Is that why you moved on so quickly?

C

ROBERT	Army No 22208092	SMITH
Enlisted Wolverhampton	On 5-7-48	ROYAL ARTILLERY
Religion C of E	Marital Status Single	Next of Kin Mrs M Gorton Relationship Sister Address 2 Old Barn Road, Anfield, Liverpool

Civilian Occupation

Military History – Service at Home and Abroad:

Iron Moulder	Theatre / Country	From	To	Years	Days
	HOME	5.7.48	9.9.48		67
	MELF	10.9.48	9.9.51	3	-
	HOME	10.9.51	11.2.53	1	155

Address on Discharge
3 Panton Road, Stoneycroft, Liverpool

Extract from military service file Army No 22208092 Robert Smith

Dear Dad,

The story goes that in July 1948 you are at a bus stop in Wolverhampton. It is 4 July, American Independence Day; Independence Day for you, too, as this is your Discharge Day, the day your army service officially ended. It starts to rain. Your bus is late.

Years later you would say it was rain and boredom that drove you into the recruiting office. If your civvies hadn't seemed to weigh heavier on you than your army uniform ever had; if you'd felt some excitement about the prospects offered by your job at the foundry; if being about to turn thirty that autumn hadn't made you think yet again life was passing you by; if the sun had been shining and the bus had arrived on time, you would already be leaving behind the streets of Wolverhampton on your way back to Liverpool, Old Barn Road and Bet. Instead you find yourself sitting across a desk from a recruiting sergeant, accepting a pen, signing up for another four years in the Royal Artillery.

It's a good story but the one question I never asked you is this: how did you come to be in Wolverhampton?

C

Dear Dad,

I found a photograph of you last night.

The stamp on the back says Ultra Studios Limited, 233 High Street, West Bromwich. You look bored. Was the sitting longer than expected?

You're dapper, though, hair slicked back, houndstooth jacket, shirt and tie, a smart young buck about to shed his civvies for the second time.

Here's what I think: the photograph was taken as you travelled from the recruiting office in Wolverhampton to the RA depot in West Brom. It was a memento, a goodbye gift for Bet.

Two months later, you were back in North Africa.

C

Part II/III Order No and Date	Unit	Personal Occurrence	Rank	Date
161 to 10 7/48	Depot RA	Attested and posted	Gnr	5.7.48
217/48	Depot	Emb UK for MELF (Cyrenica)	Gnr	10.9.48
		Disemb Benghazi & att X(IV) Drft: DBAUV		18.9.48
200/49	48 FLD	Re-classfd DVR GP C Cl III	DVR	27.4.49
496/4/49	"	Benghazi / In open arrest 6/6/69 to 21/7/49 Sec 40AA Negligently driving a WD vch thereby involving in a traffic accident, killing a horse 40AA WOAS When involved in a traffic accident did neglect to stop and find out what damage had been caused.		6.6.49
		Awarded 14 days CB		21.7.49

Extract from military service file Army No 22208092 Robert Smith

Dear Dad,
Eight days at sea; then you disembarked in Benghazi.

You never mentioned Libya. Did the posting rake up buried memories from World War Two? Did you dislike the hot, humid summers?

Or did you want to bury the story of your arrest?

Poor Benghazi! Libya's second largest city and a major seaport, so beautiful, so strategic, so coveted in the war by the Allies and Axis powers alike that both sides bombed it, fought in it, and mostly obliterated it.

The city had endured five regime changes in less than two years. Britain had captured it from the incumbent Italy, ceded it to Germany two months later, recaptured it, lost it to Germany again after only a month, until finally the Eighth Army recaptured the city in November 1942 and pursued the Axis Armies across Libya.

That was six years previously.

Call it fate, destiny, kismet, the will of God, or what you will but here you are again, this time not to capture Benghazi but to manage it. In 1948 two thirds of what is now Libya was under British military administration, with the remaining third controlled by France.

(If you didn't like being back, call it bad juju, cause and effect, karma; a man reaping the seed he sowed.)

Perhaps it was simply that your timing was off; September 1948 wasn't a great time to arrive in Libya. The first Arab-Israeli war had started four months before, in May 1948, following the proclamation of the State of Israel. Libya had no direct involvement in the war (unsurprising, given it was controlled by the British and French) but spillover riots in June 1948 in Tripoli and surrounding areas left almost twenty dead, ninety injured and three hundred homeless. There were attacks in Benghazi, too, though not on the same scale.

By November 1948 Libyan Jewish and Arab leaders told the American consul that inter-ethnic relations were better than they'd been for years – possibly a low bar to start with – nevertheless I imagine the British military would still be feeling jumpy when you arrived.

There were two British barracks in Benghazi. One, Lumsden, was small, so chances are you were in the much larger D'Aosta barracks, a former fort on the outskirts of the city, on the Benina Road; before you turned into the camp there was an Arab village.

Is that how you killed the horse?

The description on your military record is concise but compelling.

I see you speeding out of the camp towards the city, turning onto the left hand side of the road, forgetting in that moment that Libyans drive on the right, seeing (too late) a horse-drawn vehicle on your/their side of the road coming straight at you, or (more accurately) you at it.

At the moment of impact – or just before – you remembered. You should have been on the right, which meant you were in the wrong. You panicked.

What happened next...and the fallout...is that why (without saying why) you encouraged me to own my mistakes? Because it takes humility to admit you've done a bad thing and it takes courage to look the person you've wronged directly in the eye and apologise – as you never did or ever could.

You didn't stop, did you? Jesus, Dad. You: a hit-and-run driver. Is that why you erased Libya from your personal history?

You'd arrived as a gunner in September 1948 and were reclassified as a driver in April 1949. Barely a month later and you were in open arrest, from early June to late July 1949, pending investigation. Your punishment was fourteen days confined to barracks (CB) – so eight weeks CB in all, which doesn't seem so bad.

Did the army compensate the owner of the horse?

After your release you remained in Libya – still as a driver – until June 1950, which means you lived there almost two years.

What did you do there, how did you spend your free time? Did you visit the ancient ruins at Ptolemais? Did you swim in the Mediterranean Sea at the Calaque de Maubois? Did you see the desert-mountains and rock carvings at Acacus?

Despite heat and humidity, memories of war, accident and arrest, wasn't it magical? Wasn't it good at least to be some place other than cold-grey Britain when you weren't being shot at?

Two years! Why did you never mention the place?

C

Part II/III Order No and Date	Unit	Personal Occurrence	Rank	Date
2/50	36 HAA	Posted Malta	GNR	8.6.50
190/51 20 7/51	"	Emb Malta for UK (Python)	"	5.9.51
196/51	Depot AA	RHE Python		10.9.51
243 10 11/51	"	SOS on PA to MOCS (Unspecified)		9.11.51

From	To	Theatre/Country	Unit	Part II/III Order No
10.9.51	9.11.51	UK	Depot RA (CA&AA)	196/2/51 Depot RA (CA&AA)
10.11.51	7.1.53	UK	MONS OCS	III 319/51 III 8/53
8.1.53	11.2.53	UK	Y/6 List	III 8/53 MONS OCS

Extract from military service file Army No 22208092 Robert Smith

Dear Dad,

In June 1950 you were reclassified as a gunner and boarded a ship bound for Malta, where you spent the rest of your three-year overseas posting.

Wherever you'd been posted I expect you would have felt relieved to see the Libyan coastline finally fade into the horizon, but this time you'd landed on your feet.

There was only one British garrison left on Malta by the time you arrived. Less than ten years before the island had been bombarded by German and Italian forces – bombarded from the sea, bombarded from the air – to the point of obliteration and starvation. The Maltese people were awarded the George Cross in 1942 for courage; in turn they were grateful to Churchill for risking a convoy of ships to deliver food and supplies. We saved each other.

When the war was over, the islanders were happy co-existing with the British military; the British were their protection guarantee, a security blanket. But what is the role of a gunner when there's peace and a supportive population? Your duties would have been undemanding; you'd have had little to do apart from practice drills.

You'd have enjoyed the food: not only the menu but how much was available, the sheer bounty. Back home in England there was rationing, shortages, a day to day scramble to make ends meet. At Malta garrison, food was plentiful. You could have as much food and beer as you liked, and all for free.

Malta has a great climate, mild in winter, warm in summer. I visited in November; the temperature never dropped below twenty degrees Celsius and the sea was as clear-blue as the sky – a world away from the grey UK weather I'd left behind.

The island still feels British even though we pulled out sixty years ago in 1964 – or rather it provides a glimpse of what Britain might be if it was unmoored from the island of Ireland, towed south past the Bay of Biscay, hankered left and squeezed through the Strait of Gibraltar, then anchored in the middle of the Med, two hundred miles off the coast of North Africa. The island itself, which is tiny, only seventeen miles between its two farthest points, is exceedingly pretty, a rocky coastline dotted with small bays and beaches.

So after two days at sea you disembarked in Valetta. You found sunshine, bays, beaches, chocolate, cigarettes, and no work to speak of. No wonder being stationed in Malta was one the happiest times of your life.

The site of your old barracks at Tigne Point, Sliema, now houses a smart, new shopping mall, the largest on the island, called The Point. You'd recognise the portico in front of the main mall; it's the facade of one of the original buildings that made up the barracks, a series of arches and columns running along one side of the central square. I'd imagined a barracks would be utilitarian but the architectural detail in that frontage is strikingly beautiful. But for Malta's strict heritage rules, those arches and columns might have been demolished.

129

I spent an hour under that portico at an outside table of one of the cafe-bars that surround the square, drinking latte and Cisk beer, completing a crossword, people-watching, and generally having a very happy time of it. It was strange to think you might once have passed within a hair's breadth of where I was sitting.

Glass empty and crossword completed, I wandered around Tigne Point trying to find the route to the main promenade in Sliema. Your old barracks was certainly in a beautiful location, near the tip of a small peninsula, with the sea on three sides and views across to Valetta. When you talked about jumping off rocks into the sea, I imagined you seeking out cliffs to dive from, but the coastline is mostly so rocky that jumping would have been the only way to access the sea. There are now ladders at various points to aid access – and egress. If there were no ladders in your time, how did you get back out?

I can understand why you would be sad to leave Malta – if I'd have lived there I wouldn't have wanted to leave either – but the army is like the priesthood: you do what you're told, and go where you're told. Your Malta posting lasted little more than a year, then you were sent back home to the RA Depot (Civil Affairs and Anti Aircraft), just outside West Bromwich.

C

Dear Dad,

It must have been a come down returning to England after a year in the Maltese sunshine, but there was one thing, at least, where England had the edge: football; and you were posted to exactly the right part of England at exactly the right time.

The Black Country was an exciting place for a football fan in the 1950s. When you arrived at the RA Depot in 1951 the two local teams, West Bromwich Albion and Wolverhampton Wanderers, eleven miles apart, were both in the top flight, the old First Division, and about to embark on the most successful periods in their clubs' histories. You simply had to pick a side.

The first league game after you were back, 15 September 1951, West Brom were at their home ground, The Hawthorns; Wolves were playing away. Was that all it took? Or was it Albion's reputation for attacking flair that made you choose them over their vulpine neighbours?

That first home game was against Chartlon Athletic, a 1-1 draw; West Brom's next home game was a 2-3 loss to Middlesborough, followed by a 0-0 draw with Huddersfield. Not a great start. Then they found their shooting boots, putting five past Portsmouth to win 5-0, beating Manchester City 3-2, and in between slotting five past Liverpool at Anfield to beat your home city team 2-5.

Six months later you were at your first Black County derby match, one of the oldest derbies in the league, part of the forty-thousand-strong crowd at The Hawthorns giving it lally with a wooden football rattle, cheering on the Albion to a 2-1 victory. It was 14 April 1952. The very next day you were at Wolves's home ground, Molineux, doing it all over again, as West Brom thumped the home side 1-4 in front of a crowd of fifty thousand. Black Country bragging rights belonged to the Baggies. You were hooked.

Except...except...perhaps you missed the derby matches. In November 1951 you were posted to MONS Officer Cadet School in Aldershot.

What you did at MONS OCS, exactly, you never said. Was it was there you were called on to drive officers around, not post-war Italy? Perhaps it was both.

Aldershot is a hundred miles from West Bromwich. You stayed faithful to the Albion nevertheless, perhaps travelling up to the match whenever you could get a pass out. They ended the 1951/52 season in thirteenth place, three points and three places above their local rivals. The 1952/53 season was more exciting, with Albion challenging for the title, eventually finishing fourth, four points behind the winners, Arsenal. Local bragging rights went to Wolves, though, who finished one place and one point better off, having held the Baggies to a 1-1 draw at the Hawthorns in October 1952 and bested them 2-0 at Molineux in March 1953. There was disappointment in the FA Cup, too, losing 0-4 at home to Chelsea in the fourth round after the fourth replay.

Did disappointment on the pitch feed disgruntlement off it? Perhaps the posting to MONS OCS made you dream of being more than Gunner Smith all your life, moving up the ranks. Lance Corporal Smith, Corporal Smith, Sergeant Smith even. Why not? You'd served your time and knew more that the younger men with grammar school educations who were being promoted ahead of you.

Did they reject your application to the officer training programme or did you not quite make the grade? Maybe you decided it would be pointless to apply. Your orphanage background, your lack of formal qualifications...

I've read your Army Testimonial, Dad. It's glowing: honest and loyal, a willing worker, a good motor mechanic, cheerful, a good footballer, exemplary conduct etc., etc.,...but not officer material, apparently.

For the first time in your army career, you began to feel disillusioned and restless. You were thirty-four years old, considering your future. Civvie Street was calling you, promising good employment, work satisfaction, progression; a siren song that proved impossible to ignore.

C

For Better or Worse (1953 to 1954)

Dear Dad,

On 11 February 1953 you were discharged from the army under paragraph 390 (xxi)b of the Kings Regulations 1940 'on termination of his period of engagement'. This time you didn't walk into a recruitment office; you headed back once more to the only person you knew for sure would take you in: Bet.

Bet wasn't expecting you. How she reacted when she answered the door and saw you on her doorstep, without prior warning, you didn't say. Did she press you to stay? Did she assume you just needed somewhere for a night or a few days or even a week? How long did she put you up before the penny finally dropped that you weren't planning on leaving?

Bet and Richard's daughter, Thelma, was by then a young lady of nineteen; their son Reg, was twenty-two. How would Reg feel about sharing a bedroom with his long-lost Uncle Robert? (If he was still living at home; he might have moved out by then.) Did it ever occur to you that it's one thing to provide a home for your brother when he's thirteen; an entirely different proposition when your brother is thirty-four?

I might be muddling events though, merging stories. Perhaps it was in 1946 when you were released to Class Z Reserve that you arrived out of the blue; perhaps in 1953 Bet knew you were coming. You must have corresponded with her or you wouldn't have known her address. The Gortons had moved from Old Barn Road and were now living in a prefab at 3 Panton Road (another road that would be bulldozed in the 1960s) off Brainerd Street, Stoneycroft. Whether she was expecting you or not, however much she welcomed you or not in her heart, she did what any good sister would do and took you in for the third time.

You no longer asked Bet about Agnes or Barnardo's, nor did you make any move to reconnect with your three lost siblings, Nancy, Billy, and Dickie, not even to find out if they'd survived the war. It wasn't inertia or lack of curiosity; you found the idea of tracking them down distasteful. Why should you look for them when, as you saw it, they hadn't lifted a finger to get you out of Barnardo's? Only Bet had effected your escape. You had Bet and, through her, Richard Gorton, your brother-in-law and best friend; they were enough. Nancy, Billy and Dickie weren't there when you needed them; you didn't need or want them now.

Did Bet encourage you to think this way? Because it's nonsense when you think about it; Bet wrote to Barnardo's to inform them of Agnes's death and became their main contact by default. If Nancy had written that letter, or Billy, it's possible you'd have been restored to one of them. Dickie was only two years older than you and can't be considered accountable for any of it.

I'm starting to construct a theory.

Bet wasn't in touch with Nancy, Billy and Dickie (as far as we know) and didn't want you to find them. That Bet kept in touch with you but not with the other three siblings is puzzling in itself. I'm starting to believe it might be tied into the truth about Agnes. Nancy and Billy, if not Dickie, would certainly be old enough to know what happened to their mother...your mother. I'm convinced Agnes is the key to everything.

I believe this and I also don't believe it.

Perhaps it was the other way around, the other siblings cutting ties with Bet, not wanting contact. Bet registered Agnes's death, not Nancy, the eldest child, or Billy, the eldest son, as you might expect. Maybe Bet was the only one who cared enough to hold Agnes's hand as she lay dying and yours as she led you away from Stepney Clearing House and onto the train to Liverpool.

And you – perhaps at this stage in your life you were simply more interested in navigating the present and mapping out the future than you were in retreading the past. You were in your middle-thirties, living with your sister, sharing a room with your nephew, without a job or a home of your own. You needed to get on with your life, look forwards not backwards; I can see that.

By your own account Bet sorted through your clothes and got rid of anything old and shabby, including a sports jacket with a pocket where you had stowed your war medals, including the Africa Star medal, which is why I never got to see it, why you never got to show it off to me. You never really forgave her, did you? (This too could have happened in 1946. It doesn't matter. The result was the same.)

But life went on. You found work as a barman. Bet, now manageress in Scotts (or was it Gourleys?), introduced you to a work colleague, a quiet twenty-eight-year-old woman called Mary Nesbitt. Mary had been a sickly child and for a time had lived in a convalescent home, suffering similar conditions as you had experienced in Barnardo's. You had that in common, if nothing else.

Nine months later you proposed and Mary said yes.

C

Dear Dad,

Your wedding day did not go to plan.

Mum had dreamed of a summer wedding but her youngest sister, Terri, who was to be married in July, insisted the proper order of things was for Mary to tie the knot first, and her parish church was already fully booked in June. May, April, March? The priest shook his head. All late-spring dates were taken and he would not celebrate a marriage during Lent. So the date was set for the last Saturday before the start of Lent: Saturday 27 February.

Then there was the question of a dress. The priest explained that because you were not a baptised Catholic, the marriage wouldn't take place in the main church. Mum was torn; she wanted a traditional wedding gown but worried it was an unnecessary extravagance in the circumstances: no organ, no aisle, no heads turning to catch their first glimpse of her gliding to the altar; simply entering unseen through a side door and exchanging vows in the vestry. Perhaps it would be better to spend her limited funds on something she might wear again, something smart and sensible.

When she stepped out of the wedding car on the Big Day wearing a beige skirt suit, the priest was waiting with news of a dispensation granted by the Archbishop: she was to be married in church after all. That's how you and Mum became the first 'mixed' couple (Protestant and Catholic) to be married at the altar of St Dominic's Church. It was a source of pride to Mum, though pride laced with regret. She hadn't known it was possible; she felt robbed of her day in white.

Alongside compromises over the date and the dress, there was Mum's strained relationship with Bet. I can see it might be tricky to find a happy balance when your boss becomes your sister-in-law. Cracks began showing at the wedding reception. Bet asked if she could have a cup of tea, Mum got up to make it, and Terri, always a loose cannon, was raging.

Why do I know it happened? How can something so small become a story passed down to the next generation? But history turns on a sixpence. The cheek of that woman (as told and retold), expecting Mum to dance attendance on her own wedding day!

Bet's interpretation of the incident would be different, I imagine, if she even remembered it at all. She didn't actually ask the bride to DO anything. She expected Mary to delegate the job (as Bet herself would have done). Was it her fault if Mary heard it as a direct request (as would be usual at work)? Mum, despite her name, was one of life's Marthas, happy to serve; the episode might have passed unnoticed if Terri hadn't taken offence on her behalf.

Tea-gate became the magnifying glass for other perceived slights. Bet once said that if she hadn't wanted Mum to marry her brother, he wouldn't have married her – so insulting! Mum once dropped biscuit crumbs on Bet's carpet whereupon Bet fetched a dust-pan and brush and swept them up right in front of her – so rude! It's not so hard to find something to confirm a point of view.

Bet was fifteen years older than Mum and had taken care of you on and off since you were thirteen. Was Mum jealous of how much Bet meant to you? Was her relationship with Bet effectively that of mother-in-law/daughter-in-law rather than sister-in-law/sister-in-law? Whatever the reason, it probably wasn't long before you realised the two most important women in your life would never be friends.

So let's sign off on your wedding day: Mum hoping a sliver of sunlight might break through the grey winter clouds, wishing it was July and she was floating in white lace and chiffon, Bet drinking tea made with bad grace by Terri, you nervously smoking a cigarette, your father-in-law Martin Nesbitt drunk (or well on the way) and trying to engage everyone in a sing-a-long, Richard, Thelma and all the rest doing what people do at a wedding, saying how lovely the bride looks, congratulating the groom.

For better or worse on 27 February 1954, almost exactly one year after returning to Liverpool, you married Mum and moved out of Bet's home, this time for good.
C

Family (1954 to 1969)

Dear Dad,

In 1954 I expect the Nesbitt family home at 94 Finch Lane seemed relatively modern.

It had been built only twenty years earlier, part of a council estate built to house inner-city families displaced by the slum clearances, and had three bedrooms, an inside toilet, and gardens at the front and the rear. Martin Nesbitt, the head of the household, was a widower; his eldest child and only son, Robbie, was in Australia, but his three girls, Mary, Winnie and Terri, were living at home. With a bit of re-shuffling there was room for one more, particularly as the one more in question had few possessions and would be sharing a room (and a bed) with Mary.

So it was settled. Following a one-night honeymoon in The Royal Sportsman Hotel in the Welsh coastal town of Porthmadog, you would move in with the Nesbitts.

Was that how it went? It wasn't unusual for young couples to begin married life at the in-laws. Was that why it didn't occur to anyone, Mum, Bet, Richard – you, even – that you might be entirely unprepared for life at number 94?

Martin possessed a rich singing voice and a bass harmonica, and wasn't shy of showing off both, particularly when his vocal chords had been lubricated by an afternoon and evening in his local. When he rolled home, convivially drunk, as he usually did, there was generally an audience in his living room: Winnie's boyfriend, Tony, and Terri's boyfriend, Joe were constant visitors, as were friends and neighbours. Martin presided over a house with an ever open door

You on the other hand were largely institutionalised, having spent eighteen of your thirty-five years – more than half your life – either in Dr Barnardo's homes or in the Army. You were used to tidiness, order and discipline, not the cheerful mess and chaos that number 94 afforded. You had no liking for Joe, who was twelve years younger, nor even for Tony, though he was nearer your age, and it probably didn't help that Joe and Tony were thick as thieves. You disapproved of Martin's drunkenness (ironic given what came later) and were naturally excluded from the girly conversations and confidences between the three sisters.

You lacked the easy assurance to command attention and hold a room. You spoke little and were largely ignored. The Nesbitts had made room for you, but you never really fitted in. They took you into their home but never really took you into their hearts.

None of it mattered, though, because you dreamt of a different life, and that dream took the shape of Mum's brother, Robbie.

Robbie Nesbitt had served in World War Two as a seaman in the RAF, a role that involved locating aircrew whose planes had crashed in the sea, rescuing the living and recovering the bodies of the dead. His war was in the Asia-Pacific; it was there he first met Australians.

After the war, he came home to find Liverpool bombed to bits and the class system as entrenched as ever. He missed the Southern Hemisphere sunshine, the easy informality of the Aussie men; he remembered their stories of life back home. Australia, it seemed to Robbie, was a land of openness and opportunity, with sun, sea and sand to boot. It would be like living permanently on holiday.

Five and a half years after VJ Day, Robbie was on the *Dorsetshire,* a Bibby Line ship, sailing across the eleven thousand miles of ocean separating Liverpool from Melbourne.

Robbie set about gathering the necessary components to build a new life: a home, a job, friends. He joined the Victoria Branch of the Federated Iron Worker's Association and the Catholic Young Men's Society of Victoria. He worked hard and played hard. His body once more became bronzed in the sunshine. But as one year in Australia became two, then three, Robbie found himself increasingly thinking of his family back in Liverpool, the city he still thought of as home.

Robbie missed his father and his sisters. The need to see them grew and grew until he hit on what he thought was the perfect solution. Why not get them to Melbourne? Martin, Mary and her new husband, Robert, they'd love it here, Robbie was sure of it. Perhaps in time Winnie and Terri and their husbands would follow. It would be a new start for the whole family.

It seemed like it could happen. You were keen. Australia was a young country and your lack of qualifications, your lack of connections, would not weigh so heavily against you there. In Australia, Robbie assured you, a man was judged on character and capability not patrimony and patronage. Potential mattered more than parentage.

Robbie had opened a door. All that remained was to step through.

C

Dear Dad,

How long did you allow yourself to dream before you realised it would never be more than that: a day, a week, a month, a year?

Martin, widowed a decade ago, would not leave the country where his wife was buried and Mum would not emigrate if Martin stayed behind. Mary, seemingly so quiet and malleable before marriage, was unshakeable. She would not leave her father.

There would be no new start, no new life; no new country.

Robbie moved back home, sharing a bedroom with Martin.

The Australia debacle happened long before I was born; while I can't help but feel a little sad for you, Dad, and a little annoyed at Mum, that sadness is tempered by knowing I owe my life to her intransigence.

I sometimes wonder how different life might have been if I'd been born in Australia, grown up in Australia, but really I know there would have been no sun-kissed childhood for me; if circumstances had been different there would have been no 'me'. So I can't really be sad for you, Dad, because like everyone (and everyone who has ever lived or will live) we've both won the biggest lottery of them all: Life.

C

Dear Dad,

Whatever life you aspired to outside the army, I imagine your early married life wasn't it.

A wife, yes, a home; a family, yes, yes...but this? A three-bedroom house shared with four in-laws: Robbie, Winnie and Terri, dashing in from work and out as quickly, Martin rolling home, singing until all hours, and swearing like a trooper if anyone tried to make him hush; Mary fussing and flitting around to feed them all.

Bet and Richard Gorton were never far from your thoughts, I expect. You crossed the city once a week, returning to your old stomping ground to enjoy a pint with Richard. That meeting, that drink, was your oasis. Richard was a good man and a good friend. I imagine him reminding you that married life is difficult for everyone at first; that living with the Nesbitts was temporary; you would soon have your own home.

Richard was wrong on the last point – it would be many years before you and Mum moved out of number 94 – although he was right about the temporary nature of the current set-up. Life for the Nesbitt clan was in rapid flux. Five months after you moved into number 94, Terri married Joe Martinez (a summer bride, a white wedding) and moved in with her in-laws. The following year Winnie married Tony (another summer bride, another white wedding) and moved out in her turn.

So now there were five: you, Mum, Martin, Robbie...and the baby. A few months earlier, Mum had given birth to your first child, Ann Martina – Ann after Our Lady's mother and Martina after Martin Nesbitt – although from the start you always called her Tina.

(An astrologer might assert your birth-stars were aligned to make 24 April a significant date for you. It was on that date in 1928 when Dr Barnardo's moved you from Liverpool to Clapham, in 1939 when you enlisted for the TA, and in 1955 when Tina was born.)

A second child, a son, came along three years later in 1958, christened Ronald William – not Robert, after you, as intended, because Terri put it into Mum's head that having two Roberts in the family would be too confusing. (Evidently she found nothing objectionable in the boy's middle name, in memory of the father you'd never known.) The Smiths now matched the Nesbitts at number 94 at three-all (counting Mum as a Nesbitt).

You needed to provide for your growing family but your lack of formal qualifications and your years in the army counted against you. You didn't have certificates to show a prospective employer, nor years of employment with a local firm under your belt. Your iron moulding skills were out of date; at thirty-five you were considered old at the time to be starting on the bottom rung of the ladder. Unlike Richard Gorton, who over time had worked his way up to white-collar job, all you had to show for twelve years' service were a few nice words on your service record and an army driver course. On the back of that you managed to secure a job as a forklift truck driver at BICC Cables, Prescot.

It didn't pay well; even living with Martin, money was tight. You picked up overtime whenever you could, working extra shifts at evenings and weekends. Tina and Ron would generally be bathed and in bed by the time you came home. You hardly saw them.

This wasn't how it was meant to be.

Still, you clung onto a dream of a better life. Your thoughts had moved away from Australia and towards another long-held dream: a home of your own. The Gortons, who were now living in a three-bed semi in Berksewell Road, Croxteth, encouraged you in this aspiration. Your salary, although not large, would support a modest mortgage and Bet offered to lend you money towards a deposit.

In this, too, Mum proved surprisingly stubborn. She couldn't see the point of spending money on a mortgage when it cost so little to rent. She didn't foresee a time when rents would increase to become the largest monthly outgoing, or when a house could become your biggest source of wealth. She didn't factor in that you pay off a mortgage someday, whereas a tenant pays rent forever. Her difficult relationship with Bet no doubt played a part. We don't need Bet's handouts. She thinks she's better than us; she looks down her nose at us.

Drip...drip...drip. Water or stone, which is stronger? The smallest trickle can wear a groove in the strongest rock given time. Your relationship with Bet was starting to erode.

You sided with Mum and came down in favour of council housing. But obtaining a suitable house proved to be a long-drawn-out affair; the Smiths joined the bottom of a long waiting list. If Mum had thought being married with two children made her a priority, the housing officer soon put her straight. There were other, more deserving families; she would have to wait her turn. Weekly trips to the housing office to check the vacant property board ended with the same old story: that house was about to be taken, that one was earmarked for someone higher up the list. There was never any room at the inn.

Weeks turned into months, turned into years; Mum became increasingly belligerent on visits to the housing office, speaking loudly to the girl behind the counter, making sure everyone could hear. She understood there was a list but she knew for a fact her family had been waiting longer for a house than some she could name. It wasn't right; she'd had enough.

Mum in effect declared war against The System. Every Wednesday she prepared for a skirmish, rehearsing more and more arguments, taking more and more of the girl-behind-the-counter's time. The queue behind Mum became longer each week, increasingly restive or supportive depending on the general mood, which in turn afforded Mum more opportunities for engagement and more delay.

Drip...drip...drip.

The girl-behind-the-counter eventually decided on appeasement.

She offered Mum a flat with no garden, which was refused out of hand. What good was a garden-less flat to a woman with two children and another one on the way (see how quickly the years fly by)?

She offered Mum a house in a different area; it was too far from Martin.

She offered Mum a maisonette in Cantril Farm, one of the new towns springing up on the periphery of the Liverpool City Region, warning the family would be removed from the waiting list if that offer was rejected.

Cantril Farm, the name, evokes images of fields, countryside, nature; a good environment for children to grow up. When Mum visited, alone, she discovered the name bore little relation to reality: the landscape was entirely concrete.

Concrete tower blocks loomed ominously over concrete low-rise flats and concrete maisonettes. Concrete underpasses tunnelled under roads. The few shops that existed were housed in a square, concrete block.

It was as if the town planners had declared war on the colours of the natural world. There was no green grass, no brown earth, even. Cantril Farm was unrelentingly, unremittingly grey.

Back at the housing office, pushing a pram carrying the latest addition to the family (me – see how quickly the years fly by), Mum made a litany of reasons why Cantril Farm would not do: no proper shops, hardly any pavements, the impossibility of negotiating subways with shopping and a young child, the difficulty of climbing stairs with a pram. She asked to be allocated a house on the same road as Martin, number 167 Finch Lane, which she knew had come vacant

The dead-eyed girl-behind-the-counter reiterated the council's three-strikes-and-you're-off policy: if Mum refused the Cantril Farm property, we'd be taken off the housing list. Mum threatened to stage a sit-in.

Perhaps from my pram I picked up on Mum's sense of powerlessness, injustice, and anger. Perhaps the raised voices and bad-tempered exchanges upset me. Perhaps I was simply bored, or hungry, or tired, or cold. Whatever the reason, I started crying and wouldn't stop.

I howled like a banshee, screamed like a thing possessed, bawled so hard it looked as if I might burst.

And maybe, just maybe, the girl-behind-the-counter began to get an inkling of the sad reality of living in cramped conditions with a small child, or maybe she was ready to do anything to MAKE THE NOISE STOP.

Mum secured the tenancy to 167 Finch Lane. Fourteen years after your wedding day you finally had the keys to your own home. I like to think I played my part.

C

Family 2 (1963 to 1989)

Dear Dad

I worry the focus is gradually shifting towards Mum, which isn't going to tell me anything about Agnes – so let's pivot back to the Gortons.

My birth marked the end of a turbulent three years for Bet.

In January 1963, Richard Gorton dropped dead of a heart attack. He was fifty-four. You didn't have a telephone at the time; Reg came to the house that dreadful morning to break the news.

Three months later (almost to the day) Reg married Alida Van Beeke. It was too soon for Bet. She thought wedding celebrations so close on the heels of the funeral showed a lack of respect for Richard, and never forgave her daughter-in-law for not agreeing to postpone. The arrival of Bet's first grandchild, Debra, in 1965, did little to heal the relationship, particularly as the young couple had moved from Liverpool to Crewe.

The Gortons were falling apart.

You said the day Richard Gorton died was one of the saddest of your life, on a par with the day you learned of the death of your mother, Agnes. I was ten – I found that hard to comprehend. Richard had died years before I was born and, like most children, I couldn't make the emotional leap to imagine a relationship that predated my own existence.

I see now that Richard Gorton was more to you than a brother-in-law, more than a man who happened to marry your sister. He was friend, confidant, brother, teacher, father figure, role model. He was the most significant male relationship in your life.

And then suddenly he was gone.

An outsider might think Richard Gorton's death would have strengthened your relationship with Bet. As far as I can tell it seemed to have the opposite effect. In a fuzzy, ill-defined way, you blamed Bet for Richard's passing. There was talk of how Bet liked to play the lady, how Richard had done everything for her and she hadn't needed to lift a finger. The subtext was clear: Bet had worked Richard into an early grave.

(Ironically, Bet would say the same about Ada when Reg died of a heart attack fifteen years later, aged only forty-seven.)

Bet had been your anchor, your lifeline, your lodestar ever since you were ten years old. You cut yourself loose from her when Richard died; yet without her you were unmoored, adrift.

C

Dear Dad,

As a child I regarded your lack of family as a quirk, a defining feature, like your deafness in one ear, your claw hand, and your wonky nose. I knew you'd grown up in an orphanage, separated from your brothers and sisters; beyond that I neither understood nor cared to enquire about any of it, possibly because I didn't feel the lack of half of my family.

Before we moved to 167 there were seven of us, four adults and three children, living in a three-bedroom house. You and Mum were in the main bedroom, Ron and I slept in bunk beds squeezed into same room, Granddad and Robbie shared the middle bedroom, and Tina had the box room, which was barely large enough to take a single bed.

It wasn't only the sleeping arrangements that were challenging.

There weren't enough chairs in the sole main room to allow everyone to sit down together and hardly any free floor space. The situation was exacerbated whenever Terri and Winnie came to visit, as they did every Sunday. My play areas were the tiny hallway and the deep window ledge halfway up the stairs, places too small to interest anyone else.

(Even now, I can be comfortable sitting on the floor; it was once the only space I could reliably claim as my own.)

If anything I suffered from having too many people in the family, not too few.

We rarely saw Bet after we moved to 167; Thelma would drive her over occasionally. I remember those visits as stilted affairs, far removed from the chaos and hubbub of the Nesbitt-clan gatherings. Mum would serve tea and cake on her best china tea service, retrieved from a box under the bed where she kept it safely hidden. She and Bet would converse stiffly, punctuated by Thelma's laughter, which was hearty and loud, and prompted by nothing much, an attempt to jolly things along, I guess.

I don't recollect any men ever being present, you included.

Once or twice I remember being taken to visit Bet, a journey that required two buses and my best clothes. On the way Mum would school me not to be too loud or make a mess – she would repeat her cautionary story about Bet sweeping up crumbs from the carpet as she ate. She needn't have bothered. The relationship had been formalised to such an extent I wouldn't have been shyer if I was travelling to Buckingham Palace to have tea with the Queen.

Again, I don't recall you ever joining us.

I soon divined there were two camps, team-Nesbitt and team-Gorton; I put myself firmly in the former.
C

Dear Dad,

In 167 Finch Lane family life went on in a regular, predictable pattern, seeing Granddad every day, Uncle Robbie on Saturdays, Winnie and Terri on Sundays, and Auntie Bet and Thelma once in a blue moon.

Until one day, aged seven – the same age as you when you were sent to Barnardo's – I came home from school to find an unknown man sitting on the sofa being plied with tea and biscuits by Mum.

The stranger was my Uncle Dickie.

When you were admitted to Liverpool Sheltering Home, you and Dickie were young boys, seven and nine respectively. By the time Dickie tracked you down and arrived on our doorstep, unannounced, holding a piece of paper bearing our address in one hand, written in neat capitals by Janie Edwards, his employer's wife, and a weekend case in the other, you were both in your late fifties. In between: half a century of distance and silence.

It couldn't have been easy.

But you could have at least spoken to him.

The way I remember it, Dad, it wasn't your usual taciturnity, happy to let Mum do all the talking; your silence was hostile. You didn't seem at all pleased to see Dickie. No, that's not quite right...you actually seemed to resent Dickie's presence in the house.

Dickie didn't seem to notice. He was a quiet, easy-going man, content to sit on the sofa while family life went on more or less as normal around him.

You seemed unlikely siblings in so many ways. Dickie had been sent to work on a farm in Mid Wales when he was fourteen, school leaving age at the time, and worked on several different farms before making his home at Brynawel Farm, Ystrad Meurig, where he was thought of as one of the family. He spoke Welsh as his chosen language, spoke English with a thick Welsh accent, and could neither read nor write.

Physically, though, you were undoubtedly brothers. Dickie had the same blue-grey eyes as you, the same wonky nose.

You weren't the only family member to be less than welcoming to its new addition, though. When Mum telephoned Bet to share news of Dickie's arrival, Bet declined to visit and cautioned Mum not to give Dickie her address.

Mum was exasperated and incredulous that the return of a lost brother could be met with such indifference. For her, family was the most important thing in life, the only important thing in life. Strangely, Mum blamed Bet more than you, as if Bet was the lightning rod for her anger and frustration.

It acted out something like this:

[*Dickie leaves / returns to Brynawel Farm*]

Mum: Bet is hiding something, I'm sure of it. I think she knows why you were put in Barnardo's and what became of Billy and Nancy. I think she knows what happened to your mother and why the family were split up, the circumstances, more than she's letting on. (*Pause*). Why would she refuse to see Dickie if she didn't have something to hide?

Mum was prosecutor, judge and jury. The verdict was always the same: guilty, guilty, guilty. Bet's name was mud in our house.

And what were you doing, Dad, during Mum's anti-Bet volleys? As far as I remember you mostly kept your head down and turned your one good ear the other way.

That probably explains why I became firmly entrenched in Mum's camp, growing increasingly precocious during Bet and Thelma's not-so-frequent visits. When Thelma, thirty years my elder, asked if I'd call her Auntie Thelma I fired straight back 'you're not my aunt, you're my cousin'. When Bet asked what book I was reading – I was always reading – and ventured that *The Machine Gunners* by Robert Westall didn't sound like a book for a girl, I barely looked up from the page.

After Dickie's first visit, his coming to stay became a semi-regular occurrence. My world expanded with each arrival. Before Dickie, l knew only the council estate and a week in a caravan in Talacre in summer. Dickie brought farmland, fields, mountains and valleys into my life. He brought watching the sun rise on a winter morning with only his sheep dog for company. He brought music in his voice, freedom in his heart, and peace within himself.

He remained a farm labourer his whole working life until a cycling accident in 1979 left him paralysed from the waist down. He never regained the use of his lower body and lived out the rest of his days in Tregaron Hospital, near Aberystwyth. Mum and I visited a few times, though without a car it was a punishing journey. It was only then I realised how big an effort Dickie had been making whenever he came to stay. He must have wanted to find you and have blood relatives around him so very, very much.

You never went to visit him in hospital; nor did Bet that I know of.

He died in March 1986, aged sixty-nine. Thelma drove you and Mum to the funeral, accompanied by her husband, Stan. Bet was too ill to attend, which was possibly for the best, considering she hadn't cared for his company when he was alive.

Mum and Thelma locked horns over many things that day but mostly over Dickie's will, which bequeathed everything to Will and Janie Edwards, owners of Brynawel Farm. Thelma said she'd look into getting the will set aside, meaning you and Bet would inherit. Mum was indignant, threatening to show Will and Janie a letter Bet had sent years before, reiterating the instruction not to give Dickie her address.

This is Mum's version of events; Thelma might remember it differently. At any rate, the possibility of contesting Dickie's will wasn't raised again.

The disagreement, though, drove the wedge deeper, in my eyes at least.

By my twenties, my fissure with your side of the family was complete. There had been no argument on my part, no falling out; they were simply strangers to me. When I didn't invite them to my wedding it wasn't out of malice, it simply didn't cross my mind.

Do you remember your reaction when I asked you, prompted by Mum, if you wanted me to add them to the guest list? You simply shrugged.

By then you seemed as much estranged from Bet as I was.

C

PS

Reading back over this letter it might seem as if Mum turned me against Bet, which wasn't the case. If it hadn't been for Mum I doubt I'd have known Bet at all. I didn't give any credence back then to Mum's 'Bet must know more' rants – maybe neither did she – it was only Mum venting her frustration.

I wonder whether she had a point, though. Now I come to think about it, it does seem strange that Bet would cast Dickie off so lightly, particularly given the hospitality she'd extended to you when you were a boy.

Perhaps she was hurt you'd made no real effort to keep in touch with her after Richard's death given all she'd done for you, and simply wasn't willing to risk being hurt by another younger brother. Perhaps she was worried Dickie might want to move in with her permanently; he was, after all, nearing retirement age and she was living alone in a family-sized house.

Or perhaps Mum was right...and she was hiding something about Agnes.

Losing You (1970 to 1997)

Dear Dad,

I was a golden child, a little cutie with a mop of blond curls and a limpet-like attachment to Mum. Perhaps my clinginess was the reason you began spending time with me; so Mum could cook without a toddler clamped to her leg.

On weekdays when you came home from work you would sit me on your knee and teach me to read with whatever was to hand, sometimes a story book, sometimes the Liverpool Echo. the printer's ink turning my fingers black as I traced the words. I'd leave Mum's side to watch at the living room window, impatient for you to be home – because I'd fallen in love with words, and with you, the un-locker of words.

Saturdays, though, were different. On Saturdays words made way to worlds on the TV screen. This was an entirely different kind of education: Final Score, Basil Brush, and Doctor Who. I learned that predicting score draws could win you the football pools, 'Boom Boom' meant you should laugh, and that universes run in parallel, time is fluid, and altering the past can change the future.

More so than weekdays, Saturdays became our time. On Saturday afternoons while Mum was shopping, and Tina was working in Woolworths, and Ron was hanging out in record shops or jamming guitar, we'd go on adventures.

Turn left out of the gate and we'd be heading to The Yew Tree pub. Turn right and we'd be heading to The Black Horse Inn, a longer walk but close to Woolworths, where I'd get to say hello to Tina, and choose a toy, the kind of thing Mum would never have let me have: a plastic pistol, a bow and arrow, a dinky car.

You kept my picture in your wallet, only mine, only mine, affirmation as I saw it of my golden-child, chosen-child status.

So I didn't question the fact our Saturday afternoon adventures would mostly see me sitting alone on a pub doorstep with a bag of crisps and a bottle of pop.

Or that on Sundays you'd often slip away when Mum was cooking the Sunday roast, returning long after we'd eaten, too bloated with beer to eat the food Mum had saved for you.

I thought it was normal. I thought it was what all dads did.

When did it change?
C

Dear Dad,
I was six, maybe seven.

After a Saturday adventure you were watching rugby on TV; I was sprawled at your feet with a colouring book and crayons. When the match finished you turned off the TV and said you had something important to tell me.

What you told me was this: you were dying of cancer.

I remember turning back to my colouring book as if nothing had changed, but everything felt different. I didn't know what cancer meant, exactly, but I understood it was a bad thing to have, and I knew what dying meant. I remember how calm you seemed, how accepting, speaking slowly and softly as if saying yes, it was sad, but these things happen.

And then you said something that sent my mind racing even more: I mustn't tell Mum.

Did Mum not know you had cancer? Or was she not to know that you'd told me?

Would she catch cancer and die too?

Who would take care of me if you were both dead?

I must have stayed quiet, unusually quiet, throughout the rest of the day, because later that evening when Mum was tucking me up in bed she demanded to know what was wrong. At first I resisted saying anything, mindful of your instruction, but she persisted and I told her. I thought she should know. I thought she might have answers to my troublesome questions.

She frowned but said nothing for what seemed a long time. When she eventually found her voice, it was to say you didn't have cancer, you weren't ill, you weren't dying; it was The Drink talking. Then she kissed me goodnight, taking care to close the door as she left the room.

It wasn't enough. I lay awake listening to her scolding you as if you were a naughty child.

The incident was never spoken of again but something had shifted. We stopped going on adventures – from then on Mum took me shopping with her. More significantly, I'd learned three things: you'd lied to me, it was a big lie, and Drink had a voice. Over the years I grew to hate that voice. It was childish, wheedling, querulous, petty, and overbearing.

I can't remember exactly when you moved from drinking beer to drinking whisky, and from drinking in pubs to drinking at home, but from then on weekends began spiraling out of control. You would come home from work on Friday and drink a bottle of whisky. You'd drink another two bottles on Saturday and a half bottle on Sunday. You left the house only to buy more whisky – hardly moved from your armchair, not even to go to bed. No matter how much Mum pleaded or cajoled, you preferred to sit up and drink yourself into a stupor, mechanically reaching for your glass whenever you woke. Now when you didn't eat it wasn't from being bloated: it was because you couldn't remain conscious long enough to move food from plate to mouth.

The last dregs of your Sunday half bottle were usually finished by late afternoon. Then you'd drink a pint of orange squash and go to bed until mid-evening, when you'd emerge slightly subdued looking for more squash and some supper. On Monday you'd rise early for work and not touch a drop until Friday when the cycle began again.

I learned to dread weekends. The thought of Friday began to weigh like a stone in the pit of my stomach. The worse times were the stages between sobriety and stupor. As your drunkenness increased you became a child-devil in an adult body, vindictive and destructive. Mum reckoned she could predict your behaviour based on the whisky brand. I hated her for that.

When you nearly killed my dog, BJ, by setting him loose into traffic, was that Johnnie Walker's fault? That time you watched the dial on the electricity meter for an hour, then removed all the fuses from the fuse board, was Bell's to blame? Was it Black Horse who slammed Mum against the wall when she tried to stop you leaving the house to buy another bottle, or The Famous Grouse that played Don McLean's 'American Pie' at maximum volume throughout the night. (You identified with the old boys drinking whisky and contemplating death.)

I developed a rich treasury of words:

Intoxicated,
Inebriated
Worse For Wear
Under The Influence
Incapable
Pie-Eyed
Well Away
Out Of It
Half Cut

Sozzled
Bibulous
Tired
Maudlin...

That's how Mum described you. At a push she would call you drunken. The A word was never used. Calling you an alcoholic would have made it too shameful.

Because there was shame, there was so much shame – for us, I mean, not you; you seemed impervious. Every Monday Mum would try reasoning with you, nagging you, begging you, reminding you of promises to stop drinking made and broken...but it did no good. You refused to believe Mum's account of how events had played out. Your memory of each weekend was a hollow vessel, a blank page, a black hole.

I was made to promise never to tell anyone about your 'drink problem', and as the weekend drew closer Mum would remind me 'Don't upset your father'.

Secrecy and guilt: solid foundation-stones for laying the sin of the parent on the child.

Mum was powerless to stop you drinking or control your drunken rampages, was too ashamed to ask for help, and thought it beyond the pale to leave you or throw you out – she called me 'stupid' for once mentioning divorce. I needed to come up with an escape plan.

In a sense, it was you who gave me the idea. That time you told me you were dying of cancer, you'd raised Death in my face like a stick. Did you ever foresee the stick turning into a carrot? It seemed the obvious solution: you needed to die.

You never knew – how could you? – but all those times when you made sleep impossible through fear or cold or noise, I'd lie awake imagining ways to kill you. In my mind, you died countless times. I stabbed you with the carving knife when you were passed out in your armchair. I shoved you in the back and sent you tumbling down the stairs. I laced your whisky with rat poison and waited for your guts to turn to mush.

You never knew and nor did anyone else. Dreaming and doing are worlds apart; I knew that particular path, once taken, would likely ruin my life. You would win. I wasn't going to let that happen.

The closest I came was adding vinegar to your whisky glass. In my fantasy it was a practice run for the poisoning scenario; really it was more a hope that vinegar would make the whisky sufficiently unpalatable to put you off it, if only for one weekend.

You were asleep in your armchair, a half-drunk glass on the floor beside you. The glass had to be the target because you generally kept the bottle hidden. There was some jeopardy in acting; if you woke and caught me you'd lash out, I knew, and lash out hard, like you had at Mum when you caught her getting ready to pour some whisky down the sink.

I topped up the glass, put the vinegar bottle back in the kitchen cupboard, retreated to the sofa and waited.

Before long you stirred, automatically reached down; drank.

You paused; I held my breath.

'This whisky tastes funny,' you slurred, twice, and carried on drinking.

That was my first and last sabotage attempt.

C

Dear Dad,

Monday to Thursday when you were sober, things were different, you were a different man.

You'd come home from work and listen to me read, help me practice spelling, listen as I recited times tables. You'd talk me through the day's cryptic crossword, explaining the techniques and how the answers fitted with the clues. When you'd finished you'd spread the newspaper on the living room carpet, gather our shoes and polish each pair until they shone.

You taught me card games and we'd play together, just the two of us, Rummy, Whist, Black Jack. In summer when the evenings grew longer you taught me to ride a bike, running alongside holding the saddle until I was stable enough for you to let go.

When you were sober you were patient, kind, attentive, loving.

I began thinking of you as two different people, two different fathers, Dr Jekyll and Mr Hyde. Monday to Thursday you were the best father I could ever have wished for; Friday to Sunday I wanted you dead. I struggled to understand how both fathers could inhabit the same body.

I still do.

C

Dear Dad,

Your retirement in 1979 marked the middle of a pivotal year for our family: six months earlier Tina had married and I had started secondary school; six months later Ron took up a place at Warwick University; in between we moved house to 24 Dovecot Avenue. It was a fresh chapter, a clean slate, a chance to reinvent ourselves.

If we'd hoped leaving a job you'd come to hate meant you might drink less, it didn't take long before cold, hard reality hit.

Post-retirement, the demarcation between midweek and weekend ceased to exist. Monday, Tuesday, Wednesday, Thursday, Friday, Saturday, Sunday, what did it matter? They were just days, each one as good or as bad as the next. Your drinking habits became increasingly erratic; it was impossible to predict when your binges would start. Every time I turned my key in the lock I could never be sure what I'd find on the other side of the door and nor was there any way of knowing when you'd stop. Freed from the stricture of the working week, you'd go on benders lasting a week or more.

For my part I was getting older, almost a teenager, and mixing within a wider circle. I had a growing awareness that other girls' fathers mostly drank socially in the evenings, not slumped alone in an armchair in the middle of the afternoon cradling a bottle like a newborn; that other girls' mothers did not hide their Christmas sherry in the washing machine to stop their husbands downing it when there was no whisky left to drink.

With Tina and Ron gone, I'd never felt more alone. There was no one else to share the burden. Mum didn't count. I blamed her in a way – not for your behaviour, I knew she had as little control over that as I did – for staying, for suffering it, for making me suffer it, for the silence and the shame.

The A word was still taboo, as was telling anyone what my home life was like, relatives, friends, teachers, even our parish priest. Some of the neighbours must have known or guessed – how could they not when they saw you dishevelled and staggering, on your way to the off-licence on Sunday mornings? But for the most part as far as the outside world could tell we were a lovely, functioning, stable family; we never let them see that inside we were rotten, crumbling.

There were periods, though, when you didn't drink at all for months on end. Then you'd become a normal father again, a better than normal father.

When I came home from school, I'd hand you a book and you'd test me on Latin conjugations, French vocabulary, Mathematical formulae, though you had no knowledge of Latin or French or Algebra. On Saturday mornings you'd bring me a cup of tea in bed; on Saturday evenings during football season we'd settle down side by side on the sofa, just the two of us, to watch Match of the Day. You'd patiently answer questions about the players, the teams, the rules, until I grew to understand and love the game as much as you did.

Whenever dry weeks became dry months and then dry quarter-years, the cruel hope sprang up that this time it would be different, this time you would stay sober. It never was; you never did. There was always a day when my key turned in the lock and I opened the door on a glassy-eyed, swaying creature and a room reeking of whisky.

And so it went on.

I still had two fathers, and while the sober version was undoubtedly better than the drunken one, there was no getting away from the fact that it was the former who decided to reach for the bottle and take the first sip. The wall-like certainty that Dr Jekyll and Mr Hyde were different people crumbled and fell.

And so I built a different wall to keep them both out. I suppose I still loved sober-you, though my love became more guarded, less unconditional than before: you had let me down too many times. I laughed at you if you mispronounced a French or Latin word; I mocked you when you got a football fact wrong; I called you Smith instead of Dad. If you lost patience and told me to show more respect, I'd fire back that respect had to be earned.

Whenever we argued like this, Mum said it was because we were so alike. That was anathema to me. As far as I was concerned we were north and south, chalk and cheese, fat and lean.

And so it went on.

It was a confusing, dysfunctional relationship: I punished sober-Dad in small ways for the havoc wreaked by drunk-Dad. I still wished drunk-Dad dead on occasion, though more from idle habit. By then I'd hatched a different escape plan, with greater certainty of success: A levels, university, a good job, money; a home of my own.

Mum, on the other hand, was increasingly on edge. She no longer went far from home, afraid of what she might find on her return if she left you alone for too long. She would worry you'd take a tumble down the stairs and break your neck, stumble in the kitchen with a knife in your hand, or drink so much that you would never wake up. My fantasies had become her phantasms; my dreams, her nightmares.

Aged twenty-two, it was done: degree, check; job, check; mortgage, check – and soon-to-be-married to boot.

The evening before my wedding, back in my old bedroom for the final time, Mum told me to remember this would always be my home. I laughed in her face, told her she must be mad to think I'd ever move back as long as you were alive. She said nothing, but I could tell she was hurt. If I could turn back the clock I'd hold my tongue and give her a hug, but at the time I wanted to shake her. My one thought was: what the hell does she think was going on here all these years?
C

Dear Dad,

After I'd moved out I visited each week for Sunday lunch – provided you were sober. I'd phone ahead to check; if you were drunk I wouldn't turn up.

I didn't want to talk about your drink problem, to know if it was getting better or worse, or share the burden. It wasn't my issue anymore, it was Mum's. She'd made her bed...and I was well schooled in silence.

And so it went on for more than five years, in touch but not communicating, until Mum was felled by a massive stroke.

The nadir in our relationship, Dad, came that same week.

I'd driven from Wirral to St Helens to visit Mum in hospital. You were by her bedside when I arrived, holding her hand. Before I'd walked halfway across the ward I could already see you were extravagantly drunk, though it was not much past one in the afternoon. I went to find the ward sister, who received the news blankly. The hospital would not intervene unless the visitor was causing a disturbance or the patient requested it.

I'm ashamed of what I did next.

I went to Mum's bed and ordered you to leave. You resisted but Mum cajoled you into letting me drive you home.

Throughout the journey home, I screamed and raved. How dare you turn up drunk to the hospital? You were a disgrace, you were to blame for Mum's stroke, you were pathetic, a drunk, a joke. Whenever you tried to reply, the torrent started up again. I was a wild thing, a banshee, a ball of rage.

After dropping you to your door, I drove home and wrote you a letter. The venom I'd unleashed in the car was spewed onto the page, and more besides. I posted it the same day – there was no reflection, no pulling back. I still recall the closing sentence, word for word, all these years later. 'From today, forget I'm your daughter because I no longer consider you my father.' If Mum wouldn't or couldn't divorce you, then I would.

It was only later, my righteous anger burned out, that I wondered if anyone else had been to visit Mum that day, or whether she'd lain there alone, worrying about her husband and her youngest daughter, at war with each other.

Like I said, I'm ashamed.

Mum died in hospital a few months later, in February 1997, aged seventy-two.

In the weeks between her death and her funeral, that strange period of sadness, waiting, and practicalities – collecting the death certificate, registering the death, making funeral arrangements – the phone calls started. In the dead of the night or the small hours of the morning, you'd ring, drunk, asking if I knew where Mum was. I expect you don't remember. Switching off my mobile and unplugging the landline became as much part of my bedtime routine as washing my face and cleaning my teeth. When I stopped answering, you began phoning Winnie instead. She was sympathetic at first, thinking grief was driving you to drink, but soon lost patience and unplugged her phone too.

You were barely sober at the funeral; I could hardly bear to look at you.

Without Mum holding everything together the facade was tumbling down.

C

Dear Dad,

The house was too big, you said. You moved out of 24 Dovecot Avenue into a bright bedsit in sheltered accommodation managed by a housing association.

I'd visit once a week, from duty more than love, sometimes after work, sometimes at weekends, making arrangements in advance and always phoning before I set out, supposedly to let you know I was on my way but really to listen for signs you'd been drinking: an overlong pause, slurred speech, vagueness. You'd be waiting in the foyer, smartly dressed in shirt and tie, checking the time as you opened the door, telling me I was late even if it was just by a minute: I'd said eleven o'clock and it was eleven-o-one. Your flat was always tidy and spotlessly clean. I suppose it was the old soldier in you, synchronizing your watch, primped and primed, ready for inspection.

Those carefully staged managed meetings continued for four years.

How did we get from Golden Child to that?

Maybe the rot set in the day Mum picked up the keys to 167 Finch Lane. You'd waited so long for your own home, but it wasn't really your own, was it? Mum tried to make it nice but the council were shockingly lax – like when she reported a loose stair-banister and they gave her a bag of cement – and you refused to spend time and money on someone else's property.

There was discontent outside the home, too. You'd worked hard for the BICC for more than a decade but your job was a dead-end, and graduates fresh from university were getting promoted ahead of you. It was like the army all over again. Bet offered to lend you money to buy your own business, a shop perhaps. You took Mum to look at a newsagent's, a corner store with a large, airy flat where we'd live above the shop. Mum wasn't keen.

Of course, Mum always said the rot set in earlier, when Richard Gorton died. She often talked about how you weren't a big drinker in the early years of marriage, meeting Richard for a pint or two at weekends, if that. When you were sober she'd try jollying you into joining the local bowls club, anything to get you out of the house to meet people, hoping the cure for problem drinking would be found by filling the Richard-Gorton-shaped gap in your life.

Perhaps she was even right. Perhaps there was a moment when a friend could have been a catalyst for change, a magic wand tapped on a magic cabinet, and hey presto! Hyde vanishes and Jekyll stands blinking out of the darkness and into the light. If there was such a moment, though, it had long passed.

Besides, if a new Richard Gorton in your life was all it would have taken what did that say about us? Why weren't we enough? Why wasn't I enough?

Maybe I'm writing these letters to try to make sense of your side of things. Mum was the family storyteller, selecting and discarding events, sorting the strands, adding a colour here, an extra thread there, weaving and shaping our lives as best she could into some sort of coherent pattern. She had the final say on all your big life decisions: whether to emigrate, to rent or buy a house, which road to live in, whether to run your own business or stay in a job you hated. You were in denial, insisting your drinking wasn't a problem; the problem, if there was one, was our attitude to alcohol.

And I remember something else, something that happened a lot when you were teetering on the threshold of fully sober and fully drunk. You'd stick to Mum like a shadow, calling 'Mum', 'Mum', 'Mum' over and over as you followed her from room to room. It irritated me – she was not your Mum – but more than that, your voice unnerved me. It was childlike, whining: not a man trying to locate his wife but a lost little boy trying to find his mother.

Agnes.

It all points back to her.

I haven't given up searching. I will find out what happened to her.
C

Losing You 2 (1998 to 2001)

Dear Dad,

Mum had always contended that Bet knew the reason you were admitted to Barnardo's, and what happened to Agnes. Whatever knowledge Bet had was soon buried with her: she died only a year after Mum, in 1998, aged eighty-eight.

Before Bet's funeral, I hadn't seen your side of the family for decades: Thelma was welcoming; Bet's granddaughter, Reg's eldest child, Debra, and I hit it off. For the first time I felt robbed of half my family; that this too could have turned out differently.

Not long after the funeral Thelma invited you to Sunday lunch, which became a regular arrangement until the invitations stopped as abruptly as they began.

I didn't ask why. I didn't need to.

C

Dear Dad

You never think of your parents as getting old. When you started having trouble breathing, I took it for granted you would recover. Even when you were given an oxygen tank at home, even when you were admitted to Broadgreen Hospital, even then it never entered my mind that you were dying.

In the nine months before your admission, I'd seen you only a handful of times. My marriage was falling apart and in an act of self-reinvention I'd quit my job and moved to Nottingham to study for a Master's degree.

I was back in Liverpool for the Easter break, spending the vacation working for my former employer. Dan was on the opposite side of the Mersey in a rented flat – the marital home had been sold – and I was staying with my in-laws. They lived close enough to the hospital to make me think I should visit on the way home from work, at least once or twice. During those visits you seemed in good spirits.

The crisis came from nowhere. On Good Friday I was called in: you were in a coma.

The NHS is generally good at putting you back together when you're broken, but not so good at preventing you from breaking in the first place.

Take Mum. She'd visited a GP less than a week before her stroke; he didn't take her blood pressure – something that would be easy to do, cost nothing, and might have saved her life.

It was a similar story with you. Not one medical professional thought to order a routine blood test until a ward orderly noticed the quantity of water you were drinking and asked a nurse if you were diabetic. By then it was too late. A line had been crossed, a border breached. Your blood sugar was more than three times the normal, safe level, and your kidneys were shutting down. There was no going back.

Thirty years earlier you'd lied about dying; now it was really happening.

Tina was there when I arrived. She relayed what the doctor had told her about blood sugar levels and kidneys. They were moving you that afternoon to the specialist renal unit at the city's main Royal Liverpool Hospital, although it was made clear there was nothing to be done: you were being taken there to die.

Good Friday was mostly spent at your bedside with Tina and Ron in a small, private room off one of the main wards, leaving only to sleep or eat; waiting, waiting, waiting...

Life had shrunk to a bed, a man, my siblings, four walls. The wall clock ticked, its hands moved, but time had ceased to exist. Ron held your hand; I couldn't bring myself to touch you. Sitting beside your hospital bed, hour after hour, as you lay, unconscious, between white sheets, dwarfed by the paraphernalia that attend serious illness – drips, feeding tubes, stands, monitors, machines – I felt nothing.

A few days earlier I'd confessed my lack of feeling to a priest, an elderly Irishman. He explained that an alcoholic parent toys with a child's emotions, until the child learns to deaden them. He said my lack of feeling was a coping mechanism and the fact I was visiting you in hospital was all that mattered. How you act is more important than how you feel, he told me. It consoled me at the time, the elderly priest believing I was normal, not a freakish aberration. But later...

Death is slippery, unpredictable. Doctors told us you were dying but couldn't predict when the moment would come. It could be days, weeks, even months.

As Easter Saturday saw me back at hospital, and Easter Sunday, and Easter Monday, I started to feel something after all, something worse than nothing. I was bored, resentful, and impatient to be gone. I was outside myself, unwilling to move nearer the bed and take hold of your free hand, the one Ron wasn't holding, wanting it to be over and this strange limbo-like existence to end.

I tried.

I tried to remember good things about you and think good thoughts. I told myself you taught me to read and ride a bike, to love football and crosswords; that you worked day after day, month after month, year and year in a job you hated to ensure I was fed and clothed; how you instilled in me the importance of education, which was my escape route from the council estate; made me what I am.

I tried.

I think I tried.

Did I?

Did I really? Or am I airbrushing the truth to feel better about something that is hard to admit even to myself, even now, let alone to anyone else?

The truth is by day four my brain was looping a single thought:

die you bastard die you bastard die you bastard die you
bastard die you bastard die you bastard die you bastard die
you bastard die you bastard die you bastard die you bastard
die you bastard die you bastard die you bastard die you
bastard die you bastard die you bastard die you bastard die
you bastard die you bastard die you bastard die you bastard
die you bastard
die you
bastard die
you bastard
die
you
bastard
die
you
bastard
die
you
bastard
die...

C

Dear Dad,
Bank Holiday Monday came and went. Still you clung on.

Tuesday morning:
Ron called his employer to explain he needed compassionate leave.
Tina was on holiday.
I went to work.

I'd rehearsed my reasons: it would be wrong to let down my old boss at short notice, I needed the money to fund my studies, you could be like this for months and life couldn't be put on hold indefinitely, the office was only twenty minutes from the hospital. I almost convinced myself. In reality I was looking for an excuse to be out of that room.

Tuesday lunchtime:
I was enjoying my lunch break, taking a stroll along Church Street, idly browsing at shop windows, revelling in the freedom and clement weather, when it hit me like a brick wall. Not panic, exactly, more like urgency, like needing to surface when you're swimming underwater, a fundamental, overwhelming desire for air. Something had shifted. I had to be at the hospital.

When I arrived Tina said you were dead, but I knew that already. I'd felt you go.

C

Dear Dad,

The day after you died was Dan's birthday. Although separated we were still talking, trying to work through our differences, wanting the marriage to survive. He'd arranged a night out with friends – drinks, food, possibly onto a club – and wanted me there.

I felt numb, empty, bereft. I wanted to roll myself in a duvet and hide from the world. I wanted to blot out everything and everyone. Most of all I wanted you, Dad.

Dan couldn't understand it. How could I feel like that after everything I'd said, after all that had gone before? I didn't blame him. How could he understand, when I could hardly make sense of it myself? How could I find the words to explain that what I missed and mourned so fiercely, was not the man you had become but the father you might have been?

Death creates paperwork. When Tina and I returned to the hospital to collect your death certificate, a woman with a clipboard asked whether you'd carried a kidney donor card. It wouldn't help you if he had, I told her. It felt like a sick joke, considering how you'd died.

She hardly missed a beat. She wanted permission to take the bits of you they could use, your corneas, your...I stopped listening. I couldn't bear the thought of them cutting your eyes – but Tina was already nodding, yes, was already reaching for the pen to sign the consent form.

Your funeral was conducted by a chaplain to Springfield Crematorium, by chance an ex-army chaplain. He suggested draping your coffin in the Union Jack, as befits a former soldier. We – I – dismissed the idea out of hand. Since learning more about your army career, it's an immense source of regret. I think you would have liked being acknowledged in that way.

It was the least you deserved.

Five months later, my birthday; among the envelopes on the doormat, are two bearing Tina's handwriting. One contains a 'sister' birthday card, the other a 'daughter' and suddenly I'm back in your flat with Tina, sorting through your few possessions in the weeks after your death.

There's little to do, little to show for your four score years on the planet. Among meticulously ordered paperwork – bank statements, insurance policies, pension book – we find birthday cards, already written, for every member of the family with a birthday falling between April and December: Tina, Tom, Ron, me, Winnie.

We find a brown envelope containing your birth certificate, Mum's birth certificate, your wedding certificate, your army service book, and a scrap of lined paper torn from a jotter bearing a single, half-forgotten name: Agnes Hughes.

We find an official school photograph of me, aged six, in your wallet.

We don't find the letter I wrote you four years earlier. Perhaps you couldn't bear to keep it.

C

Finding Agnes (secrets and lies) (1918 to 1926)

Dear Dad,
This is the hardest letter to write.

I know why you were sent to a children's home while Agnes was still living. I've known ever since Barnardo's Family History Service sent me a copy of your admission history. The missing piece of the jigsaw is William Smith's service in World War One.

Rewind the clock, we need to go back. We need to go back to a time before alcoholism, before children and marriage, before soldiering and World War Two, before Barnardo's; before you were born, even. We need to go back to the Great War. The crowds celebrating the 1918 Armistice run backwards into their houses; the returning troops reverse-march onto ships.

Back another year, another year, a little further, nearly there.

Stop.

June 1916.

Britain has been at war almost for two years, with another two to endure. William and Agnes Smith are bringing a fourth child into the war-torn world, a son, Dickie. They now have four children, two girls and two boys, after eleven years of marriage.

By July 1916, when Dickie's birth is registered, William is a newly conscripted private in the South Lancashire Regiment. Short of fighting men to replace those who have been killed, and with volunteers drying up, a Military Service Act had been passed to bring in compulsory conscription for single men, followed a few months later by a second act extending the net to married men. William, forty, is caught.

Private William T Smith, service number 2615, kisses goodbye to his wife and four children and is sent to Mesopotamia, joining the 6th Battalion of the Prince of Wales Volunteers (South Lancashire Regiment) where they have been stationed since February, having been evacuated from Gallipoli the previous December.

Less than a year later, William is dead.

According to Agnes's deposition to Barnardo's, William Thomas Smith, South Lancashire Regiment, died of alcoholic poisoning in Mesopotamia on 15 March 1917. There's no mistake about William's death date; I've checked it to army records.

You, Dad, were born on 10 October 1918. Do you see the difficulty? 15 March 1917 and 10 October 1918: that's a gap of eighteen months.

The collective amnesia about how, where and when William died suddenly starts to make sense.

C

Dear Dad,
This is how I imagine it...

In March 1917 Agnes receives a black-edged envelope from the War Office containing a letter informing her William is dead.

His body isn't repatriated so there's no coffin, no funeral, no grave, no headstone. Agnes isn't even told the exact circumstances of her husband's death. 'Died from alcoholic poisoning on 15 March 1917 in Mesopotamia' is all she has and all she can ever expect to have.

What did she make of that explanation? Did she accept it or was she unable to believe it? I know nothing about William Smith, whether he was a good husband and father, how his war experience shaped him. Whether she believed it or not the words 'alcoholic poisoning' doubtless become branded onto her brain. They are not words she would want to share with her children or repeat to her neighbours, nor are they words she could cling to when trying to find some small consolation in the darkness. You want to think your husband died a war hero, brave and self-sacrificing, not passed out in a pool of vomit.

Worse, 'alcoholic poisoning' on the application for a war widow's pension might cause the pension to be withheld. I picture Agnes lying awake into the small hours night after night, tossing and turning long after the rest of the household are asleep, kept awake by an unrelenting voice in her head with an unvarying message. Agnes, the separation allowance, your only source of income, will stop in twelve months. Agnes, if you don't get a widow's pension...what then? What will become of your four children, how will you keep them fed and clothed and a roof over their heads? Agnes, love, you need a back-up plan.

Night after night, always the same; the voice is there in the day-time, too, although it's loudest when everything is still and quiet and there are few quiet times during the day, with the needs of four children to attend to. Days are bad, but nights are worse.

Then one day, almost as if she's dreamed him up, in walks a man called Thomas Stafford.

According to Agnes's deposition Private Thomas Stafford, one of William's army pals, visited soon after William's death. Perhaps William and Stafford had made promises to each other to visit loved ones to pass on final messages or tokens of affection should one of them not make it home. It would be natural for Agnes to find comfort in talking to Stafford, someone who had been close to William, possibly was with him when he died or could provide more information about how it happened. His visit would offer Agnes some form of closure.

After this first visit, Stafford returns. Perhaps he feels he owes it to his old pal to keep looking in on his widow and children. Perhaps eventually he even lodges with the family; some war widows took in a lodger as a source of income.

According to Agnes's statement, Stafford took her out from time to time. I try to imagine their first outing. Would it be a dance or perhaps a walk around a park? Was Agnes giddy as a schoolgirl on a first date, awkward at the strangeness of being with a man who was not William, or at ease with Stafford from the start, like they were already an old married couple?

However it was, I imagine curtains twitching on the street, voices predicting it will end in tears.

Agnes turns a blind eye and a deaf ear to the neighbourhood Cassandras. She wants to feel like a woman again, rather than a wife, a mother, a widow. More than that, she wants to look to the future with hope. She allows herself to dream: remarriage, a new father for the children, a man bringing in a full-time wage. At night, the voice in her head turns over a name, getting familiar with its weight and sound. Agnes Stafford, Agnes Stafford, Agnes Stafford.

I like to think it begins with good intentions on both sides. I like to think that Agnes doesn't set out to entrap Stafford, and Stafford doesn't befriend Agnes simply to take 'advantage' of her (as it is described in the admission statement), or – it doesn't bear thinking about – that the physical relationship was non-consensual.

By January 1918 Agnes is pregnant.

Stafford refuses to marry her.

It would have been a devastating blow. Agnes's hopes of having a male breadwinner in the house again are dashed and she'll soon have yet another mouth to feed. Worse, much worse, she's gambled her reputation and, by extension, her potential livelihood. The pregnancy puts her application for a widow's pension into further jeopardy. In 1918 sex outside marriage was regarded as immoral and unmarried mothers were shunned as deranged or dangerous, or both. This baby could destroy Agnes.

Did she think about trying to make the problem disappear? Termination was illegal but Agnes would have known that possibilities existed – limited, dangerous possibilities. She'd be risking death, a swift bleed out from a punctured womb, or the slow onset of blood poisoning. Even so, perhaps her pace slowed as she passed the house where the backstreet abortionist lived, that local woman who was known to help a woman carrying a child she didn't want or couldn't afford to keep. Perhaps in unguarded moments at home Agnes caught herself wondering if the household object she was holding might serve to bring on a miscarriage: a spoon, a knife, a candle, a broom handle. Death or ruin, should she toss a coin? Which would be better for her four children? A sharp kick inside her...make that five children.

What was it like for her, watching her belly swell, wondering how long before she would show? Did she walk along the street with her head held high, staring out any neighbour eyeing up her bulge, offering a breezy 'Good Morning' to whispered conversations, batting away insults with ready backchat? Or did she rush home in tears if a man made a lewd remark or a woman spat at her? Either way, she would have to be carved in ice not to feel hurt, shame, anger, self-pity.

What about her children? Dickie (two) was too young, but the three eldest Nancy (twelve), Bet (nine), and Billy (seven) could hardly have escaped the shockwaves from Agnes's seismic fall. They were old enough to take in the sequence of events: their father's death, the nice man arriving, staying, the creak of floorboards and bedsprings at night, whispered conversations and raised voices, the man leaving, their mother's burgeoning belly. A school playground is the cruellest place when other kids are saying your mother is a whore-trollop-tart-strumpet-slag with a bastard in the oven and asking what it's like to live in a knocking shop. I picture the girls having their hair pulled, Billy getting into fights, teachers siding with the aggressors – because children will be children and, after all, weren't they only saying what all right-minded adults were thinking?

If Agnes did consider termination, either she couldn't go through with it or it didn't work. You were born on 10 October 1918, welcomed by your four half-siblings. (I imagine Agnes's mother, Mary-Jane Lewis, would have been less forgiving, refusing contact with her fallen daughter and the bastard child.)

So now the Smith family are six.

Dad, you were born into a world at war although, in truth, the fighting was largely over. Armistice is imminent, as is the first outbreak of Spanish flu in Liverpool.

Thomas Stafford, your father, is long gone.

C

Dear Dad,

Did you know William Smith wasn't your father? You gave Ron the middle name 'William'. Would you have done so if you knew you were illegitimate, and William Smith wasn't your bloodline, a man who'd died before you were born? Would Mum have taken me to find William Smith's name on the Roll of Honour in Liverpool Town Hall if she knew he wasn't my grandfather, if he was simply another name on a wall?

If you didn't know, it follows Bet stayed silent about your real father. It's hard to be sure why she didn't speak out. Did she want to protect you, thinking the truth might hurt? Or maybe the shame of bastardy had been instilled into the little nine-year old girl to the extent that she preferred to pretend you were her full-blood brother? Perhaps she even convinced herself it was true.

Whatever her motives might have been, the dates were a problem. Your date of birth was known and non-negotiable so she was forced to conceal William Smith's date of death. She couldn't let you learn William died in April 1917 – that one fact would blow away the lie – but William Smith could feasibly have been home on leave nine months before you were born and died between then and the outbreak of peace. If she were to invent a place, a time...details might prompt questions, more questions, and...who knew where they might lead?

The trick was not to say too much.

C

Dear Dad,

According to Agnes's deposition, after William's death she received an allowance from the Army for twelve months and then from various war funds, until 1923 when she went on to parish relief. At some point she also got an affiliation order against Stafford, the precursor to child maintenance, though he never paid regularly, if at all. She took on a cleaning job one day a week. She managed to get by – just – until 1926.

Does that year ring a bell? It should: it was the year you were admitted to the Liverpool Sheltering Home.

In 1920s Britain, there was no benefits system. In the years following your birth, I imagine Agnes does everything she can to show the world she is not morally bankrupt. Believing in the old saying 'cleanliness is next to godliness', she scrubs 24 Spurgeon Street until her knees and hands are red and sore. If a bucket of hot water and a scrubbing brush could erase mortal sin as readily as it removes the dirt from a doorstep, how different her life would have been – though her sin was more a case of being born in the wrong place at the wrong time. (Were you ever called a bastard to your face? Did you know what it meant?).

In 1920 Agnes sends Nancy, then fourteen, to Kirkdale Industrial School to train as a domestic servant; two years later Bet follows her elder sister. Agnes must pay for their uniforms – I picture her pawning her wedding ring – but she calculates their weekly wages will exceed the reduction in her allowance when they leave home, and the girls will receive their board and lodging for free.

Money is still tight, though. In 1923 the war funds stop providing assistance and Agnes applies to the Poor Law Guardians. After deliberation they decide she's deserving; apart from the unfortunate business with Stafford, her character otherwise appears to be very good. The relief is conditional on weekly inspection visits from a lady of the parish. Agnes resents these visits but submits, subsuming whatever pride remains to the more pressing need of putting food on the table. She scrubs her steps until the skin on her hands is red and cracked – Barnardo's commented that the family home in Spurgeon Street 'was very poor but clean' – and battles on.

Six years pass. By 1926 Nancy (twenty) and Bet (seventeen) are both working as domestics, and Billy (fourteen) is at Holy Trinity Industrial School. Only you (seven) and Dickie (nine) remain at home with Agnes, living on twenty-one shillings a week charitable relief. This is broadly three times the weekly rent of six shillings and sixpence but probably less than William would have been earning back in 1916, even. Parish funds are keeping the wolf from the door – but not by much.

The poverty really hits home when I look back at my childhood scrapbook. When I asked what your childhood was like you answered 'rough (no shoes or socks)'.

I don't recall you telling me that, though the statement is transcribed in my handwriting. Possibly I was too young at the time to process the information. I was an active child, ticked off for running around the house in bare feet, or kicking a ball and scuffing new shoes, so if I thought at all about no shoes or socks it would probably have been in terms of liberation, freedom.

Reading it again, with adult eyes, makes me sad. I don't even have the consolation of thinking you might have misremembered because Barnardo's deposition backs you up. The Superintendent of Liverpool Branch reports the teachers at St Saviour's primary school as saying that 'the family is well known (to them)...the children have suffered from insufficient food and their clothing has always been poor, and they have had to keep away from school at times, having no boots'.

Agnes was poor, very poor.

It would have been hard for her. Only ten years earlier she had been a respectable wife and mother, with a husband who had a steady labouring job, bringing in a steady wage; by 1926 she was a widow, surviving on charitable handouts – and a lot of people would say she didn't deserve even those, given the circumstances of your conception.

Perhaps it was her knowledge of a better life that drove Agnes to persist in trying to claim a war widow's pension from the War Office.

Theoretically, she should have started receiving it in 1918, a year after William's death. William's stated cause of death, alcoholic poisoning, and Agnes's relationship with Stafford, would bring into question both William's service and whether she was the sort of woman deserving of a pension. Up to 1926 she was yet to receive one.

But Agnes continued to battle for what she believed she was due, never giving up. At last in March 1926 – success! Nine years after William's death, her persistence finally paid off. She was awarded a war widow's pension of thirteen shillings a week for herself and Dickie.

It would prove to be a pyrrhic victory. In the cruellest blow of all, the Poor Law Guardians stopped her relief in full, regardless of the fact her pension made no provision for you. (How could it? You were not William's son.) After nine long years of fighting, Agnes is eight shillings a week worse off, more than her weekly rent. The wolf was already howling at the threshold of her Spurgeon Street home; now he is about to blow the house down. She can feel his hot breath on her neck.

Agnes won't accept it. Reducing her income makes no sense; she appeals once more to the Guardians. The Guardians are not entirely blind to the logic of her argument, although they see it the other way around. The Guardians have a plan for reducing Agnes's outgoings, also logical in its own way: if her pension makes no provision for her youngest child, that child – you, Dad – should be removed from the family home and cared for in an institution.

As I write this I try to remind myself that the Guardians were not evil people; they were not trying to punish Agnes – or you, for that matter. I try to remind myself that they truly believed they were doing the right thing.

The Guardians were products of their time, conditioned to see poverty as a moral problem. Thomas Stafford, your putative father, was known to them. This would not have helped Agnes's case. Stafford had not worked since he left the army and was lodging at a Salvation Army hostel, in receipt of parish relief himself; the Barnardo's admission report describes him as 'lazy and drunken'. The Guardians would have no qualms about taking the illegitimate child of a wastrel father from a lower category of widow. In their eyes removing the child from the family would break the cycle.

Agnes didn't give you up without a fight, Dad, you ought to know that.

She was under intense pressure, and facing ruin, but even so she refused to comply. There was no doubt in her mind you belonged with her; she told them to go jump...she would not surrender you.

Three months passed, three long, agonising months, before Agnes capitulated – as they knew she would.

She is worn out, sick and hungry. She can't fight the system forever. She has run out of time and options.

She has no choice.

The day Agnes signs you over to Barnardo's, Stafford owes her more than forty-five pounds in affiliation arrears (about three-and-a-half thousand pounds today). If he'd managed to start paying Agnes the weekly affiliation allowance of seven shillings and sixpence, even, you might not have ended up in care.

C

Dear Dad,

What was the parting like? You never talked about it. Did Agnes put on a brave face for your sake, was she hysterical, or did she simply have no more tears to cry? Did she tell you you'd only be gone for a short time? Did she manage to convince herself it might even be true?

Most of all, how do you make a seven-year-old understand they have to leave home, signed over to the care of strangers, while their nine-year-old brother is allowed to stay at home with Mum?

And I think about that 'bright…but delicate' boy. I hold him up to light and examine him like a precious jewel or an objet d'art.

I see that whatever is said or not said on that day, the boy believes his mother cannot afford to keep both him and his brother, and she has chosen to keep his brother.

He loves his mother; he cannot bring himself not to love her, so he decides to hate his brother. And he wraps the love and the hate in two sheets of paper, one a small square, about the size of two postage stamps, on which the boy writes 'Agnes Hughes, My Mum's Maiden Name', the other A4-size, on which his daughter writes 'From today you should forget I'm your daughter because I no longer consider you my father.'
C

Dear Dad,

It says on the admission statement that Agnes was in poor health when she signed you over to Barnardo's. That isn't particularly surprising, because by 1926 she'd been living in poverty for almost a decade.

But the day you were taken from her, I believe something within her finally broke, her spirit, her fight, her life-force, her will, whatever it is you choose to call the essential something that makes a person able to wake up and face another day, to keep putting one foot in front of another no matter what.

And the thing that broke in her, I believe it could never be fixed as long as she remained separated from you. Because your removal wasn't something Agnes experienced once, an isolated event disappearing further and further into the past. No. Every single day your absence would hit her the moment she woke up, bang, like a punch in the stomach, hollowing her out. Every single day she'd be a shell of a woman, weighed down by the you-shaped hole inside her. Every single night she'd dream that life was normal, you hadn't been taken away after all...but every night gave way to day. And every single day, the moment she woke up, bang, it would hit her, the knowledge you were gone.

On and on and on and on and on...yesterday, today, tomorrow and forever...You were taken from her every day, the wrench of parting happened every day. She would see the naked misery and confusion on her youngest son's face every single day, for the remaining three years of her life.

I might have got her wrong my whole life. Maybe Agnes did die of a broken heart after all, but not because you were naughty; because you had been taken from her.

The truth is, Dad, Agnes loved you very much.

Perhaps that's all you ever needed to know.

C

Dear Dad,

In a parallel universe Thomas Stafford marries Agnes. He loves his wife and his son and is kind to his four step-children. He works as a general labourer, as William had done. Thomas and Agnes grow old together. In this universe you don't go to Barnardo's or live with Bet or meet Mum. I don't exist.

In a third universe William survives the war in Mesopotamia and returns on leave in December 1917. Agnes gives birth to their fifth child in October 1918 but it is not you. In that version you don't exist either.

In a fourth universe Bet sits you down when you first go to live with her, aged thirteen, and explains it all, tells you how much you were loved, how much you were wanted. You are sad and angry but you don't feel compelled to dive to the bottom of a whisky bottle, chasing a mother's love. You meet and marry Mary Nesbitt. That's the version I like best, the one I would have been happy in.

C

Half a Family

Dear Dad,

You never tried to trace Nancy and Billy. The way you saw it, they'd abandoned you in Barnardo's; your record book doesn't show any letters or other contact from them.

So I'm going to try in your place.

Nancy.

Your Barnardo's admission statement indicates Nancy, then twenty, was working as a domestic in Oxford Street, Liverpool, earning ten shillings per week. By 1939 according to the National Register she was a live-in housemaid in The Chine Hotel, Bournemouth. I tried to find out where she went from there, if she married, but it's like looking for the proverbial needle in the proverbial haystack. In 1961 an Agnes (Nancy) Smith was married in nearby Poole to David McGuiness but the marriage certificate proves it's not your sister. Bride-Agnes was too young; her father's name was not William Thomas Smith. Your Nancy might have married outside Bournemouth; she might not have married at all. Without certainty over whether her surname stayed as Smith or changed to something else, the trail runs cold.

So I changed tack. If love didn't draw Nancy from Liverpool to Bournemouth might it have been wanderlust – and could she have been drawn even further afield? Emigration records show an Agnes (Nancy) Smith stating her occupation as maid and her birth year as 1906 setting sail from Southampton to New York in May 1948. A deeper trawl shows she worked at the Isolation Hospital in Southampton; not a definite match but possible...a definite possibility.

I imagine my half-aunt, aged forty-two, standing on the deck of the SS *Washington* watching Southampton docks fade from view, then turning away from the Old Country to face the North Atlantic and the New World.

Billy.

Searching for Billy is even more problematic if anything. He was fourteen when you were admitted to Barnardo's and had also been sent away from home, to the Holy Trinity Industrial School in Toxteth, Liverpool. The school's broad purpose was to train pauper boys in tailoring, shoemaking, joinery, or printing, skills that would set them on the path to earning a wage, so they wouldn't be a burden on society. It was a kind of boys-only borstal. Billy would have remained at Holy Trinity until he was sixteen. And then...where?

By 1939 Billy was living in 18 Aubrey Street (another street that didn't survive the 1960s clearances) off Everton Road, across Breck Road from your childhood home in Spurgeon Street, and was working as a general labourer, like his father. It wasn't a protected occupation so we can assume he was conscripted. Five thousand five hundred and sixty-four men named William T (Billy) Smith served in the armed forces in World War Two; more than three thousand William T Smiths emigrated from Liverpool after the war. My half-uncle could be any one of them.

But I persevere, spot a death registered in 1957, and order a copy of the death certificate. Name, age, occupation, area: it all fits. Billy died of a heart attack aged forty-six. He was living in Norwood Grove, Fairfield, only a mile from Panton Road, where you lived with the Gortons from 1953 to 1954, on opposite sides of Newsham Park. You might have passed each other in the street, or rubbed shoulders in a pub.

Even while Mum was encouraging you to search for Nancy and Billy, they were already far beyond your reach.

And what of your true father, my true grandfather, Thomas Stafford?

Your admission report states that in 1926, aged forty-nine, Stafford was living in a Salvation Army hostel in Park Lane, Liverpool. Trying to trace him at the hostel and beyond proves to be a dead end. The hostel's records from that time have not survived; the building itself has gone, too. All that remains of the Park Lane hostel is a photograph of an austere four-storey building, reminiscent of a warehouse, with 'The Salvation Army Working Men's Home' painted in white across the frontage. A handful of men are outside on the pavement, in the doorway, or leaning against the building, hands in pockets. They are not posing for the camera, though from the way they are staring down the lens they clearly know they are being photographed.

I look from one to the other, trying to picture my grandfather among them. They seem lacking in purpose but none are obviously lazy and drunken, as Stafford was described. Most are smartly dressed, some in suits, some in overcoats and trousers, some wearing trilbys.

According to the admission report, Stafford had never worked since leaving the army at least eight years prior. He was in receipt of parish relief. There's a chance he turned his life around, though I think it's unlikely. It's more likely that whatever demons he was trying to drown floated like corks while he himself sank further and further into a bottle.

After 1926, he disappears.

When I started these letters I wanted to find Agnes, and I've found her, but I've also learned how much has been lost. Nancy, Billy, Stafford...did their lines end or are their descendants out there somewhere? Is this it or is there still half a family somewhere waiting to be found?

In an ideal world this letter would end with tales of relatives discovered, contacts made, meet-ups, perhaps even a party, but real life is messy and complicated. The time to start looking for answers was forty years ago; now there's no one left alive to ask.

C

Dear Dad,

One of the demons Stafford was trying to drown perhaps took the shape of his old army chum, William Smith. He might have witnessed William's death or, if not his, then certainly the deaths of others. Stafford would have witnessed death and dying close up, over and over again. He would have seen it, heard it, smelt it.

William Smith was not my grandfather. I'm finding it hard to adjust my mind to that after all these years and so I find myself back at where the story began, with World War One and William, trying to unpick a mystery within a mystery.

According to Agnes's statement, William died of alcoholic poisoning, which is puzzling. How is it possible that a frontline soldier lays hands on that much alcohol?

C

Dear Dad,

Private William T Smith, service number 2615, of the 6th Battalion of the Prince of Wales Volunteers (South Lancashire Regiment), died on 15 March 1917, four days after he helped drive the Turkish Army from Baghdad.

For four days before the Turks fled, fighting was fierce and brutal. Those ninety-six hours must have been hell. When the 6th Battalion of South Lancashire's, or what was left of them, entered the city, they had been in action for more than twenty-four hours. William could have been badly wounded in the battle, he could have been exhausted by the effort and the heat; he might have been suffering from a tropical disease, like dysentery or malaria. There would be no real medical care. Treatment in the field was rudimentary and army medics often resorted to rum to treat all manner of things: wounds, shellshock, exhaustion, hypothermia, flu, dysentery. If William was seriously injured, or seriously ill, army medics could have filled him up with booze and let him take his chances.

There is another possible, less heroic explanation...

The British Army by all accounts had a tradition of supplying soldiers with alcohol. Drunkenness was not tolerated at the front line but officers turned a blind eye if troops on leave drank to excess whenever excess alcohol was available – which could happen if fighting had been fierce, a battalion decimated, and their allotted rum ration divided between far fewer men.

When the 6th Battalion entered Baghdad, they were welcomed into the city by a population glad to be rid of the Turkish Army. Crowds lined the streets and crowded onto balconies and rooftops, cheering and clapping. Women were dressed in their holiday dresses. Groups of schoolchildren danced. Perhaps William, buoyed by the joy of the people, got his hands on enough booze for a three-day-long bender; a party to end all parties.

It doesn't matter now; however it came about, the end was the same. William died separated from his wife and children, thousands of miles from home, in a hot and dusty alien land. There is no way of knowing where his grave is, or if he even has one. The only remaining trace of Smith, Pte William Thomas, 2615, is his name on the Basra Memorial in Iraq. The Memorial, maintained by the Commonwealth War Graves Commission, commemorates the 40,640 casualties of the Mesopotamia campaign. FOURTY THOUSAND SIX HUNDRED AND FORTY – that's in Iraq alone.

You can do an online search of the Basra Memorial or the Iraq Roll of Honour (whichever you prefer to call it). Alongside William's name are the names of other William Smiths who never made it home:

SMITH, Private William, 2nd Battalion Royal West Kent Regiment, 28 April 1916;

SMITH, Lance Sergeant William, 1st Battalion Oxford and Buckinghamshire Light Infantry, 22 November 1915;

SMITH, Driver William, 82nd Battery Royal Field Artillery, 31 October 1916;

SMITH, Private William Charles, 7th Battalion North Staffordshire Regiment, 25 February 1917;

SMITH, Private William George, 1st/4th Battalion Hampshire Regiment, 16 July 1915;

SMITH, Private William George, 5th Battalion Wiltshire Regiment, 25 January 1917;

SMITH, Private William Henry, 9th Battalion Worcestershire Regiment, 25 January 1917;

And (immediately above William Thomas)

SMITH, Private William Hill, Battalion of the Loyal North Lancashire Regiment, 9 April 1916.

That last name belonged to a boy aged only seventeen.

They are the men who looked at me from sepia images. They are the doomed youth who spoke to me through poetry.

They are not my grandfather.

C

Dear Dad,

A few years before you died, a counsellor asked me to name the most significant person in my life. I told her my husband. When she suggested it might be you, I was dismissive.

Definitely my husband, I insisted, there was no room for doubt.

Yet when I solve a crossword, Dad, you at my shoulder; when I watch football, you are by my side. When I remember how lucky I am to live in a nice area, in a nice house, filled with nice things, I think of you encouraging me to work hard at school, get a good education, something you were denied, and I wonder: are you proud of your little girl?

When I feel like a drink, I think of you, too. Some evenings I open a bottle of wine to prove to myself I can stop at one glass, or two, or at least won't finish the bottle. Some evenings it's harder to prove than others. (Are you proud of your little girl?)

You shaped me, Dad, for better or worse.

Except in one respect I'm nothing like you. I never wake up wanting alcohol for breakfast.

C

Dear Dad,

Agnes was your unfinished business. This book is mine.

I booked into the Art School Restaurant, in the ground floor of the former Liverpool Sheltering Home building, with Dan and two friends. We ate in the main Lantern Room dining room, which is built on the former playground of the old home. I'd brought the Barnardo's photograph to match the image to the room; the entry route into the dining room from the small bar area would have been a window of the main building looking onto the playground.

I tried to conjure up children playing, 1926-style, but the polite hubbub of fellow diners stayed just that. There were no ghosts, only gourmands and good food: five courses comprising olives with English sparkling wine (glass of), amuse bouche, cheese soufflé, lamb, and a trio of desserts.

What would you (the boy, the man) have made of it?

That fancy meal wasn't with newly acquired relatives – but it was still a catharsis of sorts.

As is this book. It's a letter to you, Dad; very different to the bile filled letter I wrote all those years ago.

I think of you every day. It's hard not to. Whenever I look in the mirror you stare back: with your wonky nose; your grey-blue eyes.

I can't rewrite the past or change history but I can do this:
Thank you.
I'm sorry.
I love you.

Somewhere, somehow, I know you can hear me.
Your daughter,
C
xxx

POSTSCRIPT

There were times during the writing of this book when I began to imagine, like the Astronomer in Rasselas, that somehow I'd acquired power over planets, or at least, power to shape world events.

I was researching the 1918 Spanish flu epidemic, when the World Health Authority declared a global pandemic for COVID-19.

I'd barely finished the chapter dealing with Dad's World War Two service when Russia invaded Ukraine and made war in Europe a real threat once more.

I was learning that Dad served in Libya during the first Arab-Israeli war while the UN were grappling with Hamas attacks on Israel and Israel's bombardment of Gaza.

With every book I opened, History was escaping off the page and rewriting itself for the 21st century.

On a more personal level, though, the opposite seemed to be true.

A blood pressure crash caused me to faint and face-plant into a cabinet, leaving me with a broken nose and a displaced septum that required surgery to fix. So I no longer see Dad's wonky nose when I look in the mirror; my nose is newly reshaped and straight.

I did though finally get to see and hold Dad's medal, the Africa Star with the Eighth Army Clasp, or if not his, exactly, then one exactly the same. My husband Dan sourced a medal online and bought it for me.

Finally, I should add something about Dad's half-niece Thelma, who disappeared from the 'letters' shortly after Mum's funeral. My siblings and I lost contact with Thelma in 2001, soon after her husband Stan died (which was the same year we lost Dad). Land Registry records and electoral rolls show she sold the marital home five years later and bought a flat in the same area, selling that in 2011. Then she, too, disappears.

I enlisted help from the Salvation Army's family tracing service but after a year they ended their investigation, having tried to make contact by various means with someone whose details match without reply or return.

At the time of writing Thelma would be in her eighties; I've accepted she doesn't want to be found or is beyond finding.

CHRONOLOGY

Year	Family	General
1879	Agnes Hughes born?	
16 Apr 1905	Agnes Hughes marries William Thomas Smith Move from Smeaton Street to Hibbert Street	
2 Apr 1906	Agnes Smith junior born (Nancy) Move to Bismarck Street	
1 May 1909	Mary Elizabeth born (Bet) Move to Spurgeon Street, where they stay	
7 Nov 1911	William Thomas Smith junior born (Billy)	
28 Jun 1914		Archduke Franz Ferdinand is assassinated
4 Aug 1914		Britain declares war on Germany
January 1916		Conscription imposed on single men aged 18 to 41
May 1916	William Thomas Smith conscripted	Conscription extended to married men
24 Jun 1916	Richard Smith born (Dickie)	
Dec 1917		Food rationing introduced
Jan 1918		Spanish flu epidemic begins
?	William Thomas Smith dies	Spanish flu in Liverpool
10 Oct 1918	Robert Smith born	

Year	Family	General
11 Nov 1918		World War One ends
1921		Rationing ends
4 May 1926		General Strike begins
12 May 1926		General Strike ends
?	Agnes dies	
2 Jun 1926	Robert to Liverpool Sheltering Home	
24 Apr 1928	Robert to Clapham home	
7 May 1928	Robert to Hove home	
16 Sep 1929	Robert to Clapham home	
29 Oct 1929		Wall Street Crash – The Great Depression begins
24 Jan 1930	Robert to Jersey home	
20 Dec 1930	Bet marries Richard Gorton	
23 Oct 1931	Reginald Richard Gorton born (Reg)	
12 May 1932	Robert to Stepney Receiving House	
13 May 1932	Robert moves in with Bet, Richard and baby Reg	
Summer 1935	Thelma Dorothy Gorton born (Thelma)	
30 Sep 1938		Chamberlain signs Peace Pact with Hitler
24 Apr 1939	Robert enlists for the TA in Wimbledon	
1 Sep 1939	Robert called out for full military service	
3 Sep 1939		Britain declares war on Germany
Jan 1940		Food rationing begins
27 May 1942	Robert serves in North Africa	
11 July 1944	Robert serves in Italy	
22 Dec 1944	Robert is wounded	
28 April 1945		Mussolini executed
29 April 1945		Hitler commits suicide

Year	Family	General
8 May 1945		Germany surrenders / VE Day
7 Jun 1945	Robert re-enlists for three years	
15 Aug 1945		Japan surrenders / VJ Day
1 Sep 1945	Robert is detrained at Milan cathedral	
6 Jan 1946	Robert is sent back to the UK	
17 Apr 1946	Robert is released to Class Z reservists – moves back to live with Bet and Richard Gorton	
4 May 1948	Robert is released at end of contract	
5 May 1948	Robert re-enlists for four years	
14 May 1948		Israeli Declaration of Independence
15 May 1948		First Arab-Israeli War begins
10 Sep 1948	Robert posted to Cyrenaica (in modern Libya)	
18 Sep 1948	Robert disembarks in Benghazi	
6 Jun 1949	Robert in open arrest	
21 Jul 1949	Robert sentenced to fourteen days confined to barracks	
8 Jun 1950	Robert is posted to Malta	
5 Sep 1951	Robert is posted to UK	
10 Sep 1951	Robert arrives in UK - posted to RA depot	
10 Nov 1951	Robert is posted to MONS OCS	

Year	Family	General
11 Feb 1953	Robert is discharged and moves back to live with Bet and Richard	
27 Feb 1954	Robert marries Mary Nesbitt and moves in with the Nesbitts	
24 Apr 1955	Ann Martina Smith is born (Tina)	
9 Aug 1958	Ronald William Smith is born (Ron)	
17 Jan 1963	Richard Gorton dies aged 51	
? 1963	Reg marries Alida Van Beek	
25 Sep 1966	Catherine Marie Smith is born (C)	
Summer 1968	The Smiths move to 167 Finch Lane	
Summer 1970	Thelma marries Stan Lovelady	
	Dickie traces Robert	
Autumn 1978	Reg dies aged 48	
Easter 1979	Robert retires	
	Dickie is paralysed in a cycling accident	
4 Aug 1979	Tina marries Tom Threlfall	
28 Mar 1986	Dickie dies aged 69	
2 Sep 1989	C marries Dan French	
15 Feb 1997	Mary dies aged 72	
Spring 1998	Bet dies aged 88	
17 Apr 2001	Robert dies aged 82	

ACKNOWLEDGEMENTS

This isn't a book with footnotes or a proper bibliography but it does depend for a large part on research conducted by others.

In this format it isn't possible to acknowledge all debts properly but I would like to note my dependence on Stephen McGreal for his work on Liverpool in the Great War, Andrea Hetherington for her work on British Widows of the First World War, Peter Higginbottom for his work on Children's Homes, and Robert Neillands for his work on the Eighth Army 1939-1945.

Various institutions have provided information and assistance, including Barnardo's, the Army Personnel Centre, and the Salvation Army. In particular I would like to thank Barnardo's for allowing me to use the photographs of Liverpool Sheltering Home, Teighmore, and Dad's restoration photograph within the sections 'Barnardo's, Liverpool' and 'Clapham and Jersey'; and the Salvation Army for permission to use the photograph of their Park Lane Hostel in the section 'Half a Family'.

I would like to thank my friend Aidan Whitehead, for setting me on the path to tracing Nancy and Billy, when I had given up hope of ever finding them.

Finally I want to thank my husband, Dan. He was my first reader and provided invaluable challenge to my first working draft His insight and questions made me reshape what I had done up to that point, and the structure and contents is better because of his input.

ABOUT THE AUTHOR

Cathy French was born and brought up in Liverpool and now lives 'over the water' in Wirral. She is a writer, publisher, and blogger. As well as fiction and memoir, she has authored a poetry collection *Love and the Spaceman*. Her book review blog is whatcathyread.com.

Printed in Great Britain
by Amazon

59091841R00142